Karen Anand was born in Mumbai, [illegible] London and was educated in England and Paris. 'Karen's' is her brand label of gourmet food products. She heads a catering company and has co-authored the best-selling *Foodlover's Guide to India Nepal.* She is European food consultant to various five-star hotels in the country and has also anchored *The Good Food Guide* on Star TV.

Praise for Lean Cuisine Curries

Healthy and worth it at the same time? (Here's) an answer
Ranjona Banerji, *Sunday Mid-day*

Definitely the book of the '90s
Ashish Virmani, *Afternoon Despatch & Courier*

An innovative, refreshing cookbook
Society

(I'd) certainly recommend *Lean Cuisine Curries* to any enthusiast of good food. I plan to use the book regularly
Sabina Sehgal Saikia, *The Times of India*

(Karen) is one of the most capable exponents of lean cuisine
The Sunday Observer

You've gotta buy the book!
The Times of India

The book is pleasantly and informally written. I am pleased I got to read this well-illustrated book which I shall treasure.
Afternoon on Sunday

To Helen,

With fond love

Noreen

A lot of these recipes are just terrific.

Oct 99 Madras

LEAN CUISINE
Curries

for Noreen
Bon Appetit
[illegible]

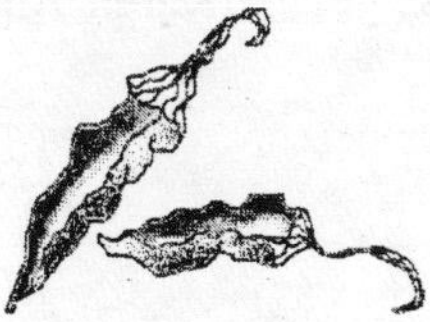

Karen Anand

Illustrations by
Urmilla Deshpande

HarperCollins *Publishers* India

The publishers would like to acknowledge with thanks the support of Jet Airways Pvt. Ltd., and Indage (India) Ltd.

HarperCollins *Publishers* India Pvt Ltd
7/16 Ansari Road, Daryaganj, New Delhi 110 002

First published 1998 by
HarperCollins *Publishers* India
Second impression 1999

ISBN 81-7223-336-1

Lean Cuisine Curries is typeset by
Arrt Creations
45 Nehru Apartments, Kalkajee,
New Delhi 110019

Cover Pictures: Urmilla Deshpande &
Design: Arrt Creations

Typeset in Garamond

Printed in India by
Gopsons Papers Ltd
A-14, Sector 60
Noida 201 301

All human history attests
That happiness for man — The Hungry Sinner!
Since Eve ate Apples, much depends on dinner.
Lord Byron, *Don Juan* 1821

To all the men in my life who have helped me bring about this book
(Fortunately or unfortunately, they happened to be men)

They tasted, told, typed and commented. They raised eyebrows and found ways of politely rejecting or happily accepting.

I cooked, they ate.
I slept, they typed.
I typed, they corrected.
I screamed, they cooked.

Thanks for your honesty and your devotion Pogo, Sasha, Wilfred, Sanjay, Amol, Rakesh and Yadu

Contents

Introduction

I grew up in London in the sixties and seventies with a mother who cooked because she had to, not because she wanted to, and a father who never entered the kitchen except to eat. Both, however, had one thing in common — they loved and missed Indian food. My father talked endlessly of hot, crusty brunes with lashings of cream from the top of the milk, which he used to eat at Irani cafes in Bombay. He drooled at the mere mention of 'kheema gutli' and 'bun chop', favourites at St Mary's, the school he went to in Byculla. St Mary's must have been one hell of a place if you can still remember what you ate there after forty years. He talked about the salt beef his mother used to make, of Christmas cake when he, as a child, had to stir the blessed thing for hours in the days before mixers, food processors and blenders. He missed kebabs and biryani and balchao and bhel. He missed what he called 'tart' — raw mangoes at the onset of summer, tamarind from the street carts parked outside the school and sour bora or dry ber, brown berries sprinkled with rock salt. He had very clear ideas about the food he liked and disliked, the nostalgia made all the more potent by the lacklustre of the English table.

He used to make sneak visits to Wembley for chivda (flattened rice with spices, which he called 'chura') and the Indian butcher, Mr. Sheikh. He kept us stocked with real mutton or goat so that my parents didn't have to eat lamb which they found smelly and insipid. My father would wait patiently for my mother to run out of basmati rice or fresh coriander so that he could drive to Southall (which was quite a long way off) to get our favourite sweetmeats — chum chums, gulab jamuns and chocolate barfi. The basmati served as a good excuse. As children, we were well acquainted with

Indian food, but ignorant as to its background and history.

My mother confused our culinary heritage further. She grew up in a half-Parsee half-Goan household without much spice. You can imagine the chutney of cuisines and cultures there! But it was Bombay's restaurants that made those eyes of hers sparkle. Bombellis at Breach Candy and great Continental food at Gourdon somewhere near Churchgate, Chinese at Nanking's behind the Taj and lobster thermidor at The Little Hut at the top of The Ritz. She experienced Bombay in its heyday. When she married my father, the fun continued, the cooks walked in and she never needed to step into the kitchen — not, that is until she reached England. My parents are like chalk and cheese in many areas, but where food is concerned their tastebuds remain united in their thorough dislike of English food. They found it bland, boring and tasteless.

Consequently, we were brought up on a strange mix of European looking dishes which tasted Indian, and Indian 'curries' which were mostly red, thick, oily and although they tasted very good, they all tasted the same. There was no distinction between, say the punch of a rogan josh or the subtlety of a fish caldin. It was mutton curry, beef curry, prawn or chicken curry. My mother rarely made fish curry in England because she said the fish had no taste. She used ginger-garlic paste and fried onions with gay abandon. She opened packets of coconut cream with great finesse and she soon discovered a miracle marriage saver called Kashmiri masala made by the pickle people, Pathaks. This was the answer to all her problems, the cure-all and the ultimate 'must' in every Indian dish, whether it was dal, vegetable or pork chops. It had about as much to do with Kashmir as my left toe. There was no trace of dry ginger powder, fennel seeds or mustard oil, the spices associated with Kashmiri food. These were replaced by the old favourites ginger, garlic, a few spices like cumin and coriander and of course, and so the name undoubtedly, ground Kashmiri chillies.

Hence, my early memories of Indian food were not very defined and certainly not based on any real knowledge in the intellectual sense. My mother had and still has a great 'hand'. She makes very authentic batata vadas and excellent puris. She always cooks rice, even now, in an aluminium handi with a tight fitting lid and the rice always comes out perfect, but she can't roll a roti to save her life. That is something you learn very early on or not at all. I am not adept at roti-making either. She puts things together in a matter of minutes and can set an extraordinary table, mainly courtesy Marks and Spencer's and the local baker, but what the hell, it all tastes fantastic and it comes from the heart. I, therefore, and understandably, grew up not knowing a papad from a pomfret.

In those days, the Indian communites in London were well established. The Gujaratis in Wembley, Sikhs in Southall and Bangladeshis in Brick Lane. But food tasted the same almost everywhere. I remember eating tandoori chicken on Ealing Road in Wembley, sev batata puri in Southall and greasy meat curries in Brick Lane. Indian food in London was, in short, a hotchpotch, the only common denominator being spice. So you grew up not really being aware of regional styles and variations, of religious customs and cultural norms, of climate and class differences. It was as if all the Indians were transported to England in one big plane and then began to learn to cook once they got there. The masalas all tasted the same, only one type of rice was ever used and there was no mention of types of chilli (you either used red or green) or the subtlety of different spices — basmati and ginger-garlic paste ruled the day.

After I finished school, I went to Paris to study and my tastebuds were awakened. I learned as much about French literature and language (the course for which I enrolled at the Sorbonne) as about food - which soon became my favourite extra curricular passion. 'Cuisine' was a heavy part of my syllabus and I had excellent teachers — a wonderful and dedicated nanny from Lyons who cooked in the style of Bocuse — classic, traditional French; the bohemian journalists with whom I lived who had a penchant for quality dishes and extraordinary wines. Krug champagne was a family staple and it was not until I walked into a wine shop years later to try and buy a bottle did I realise the value! There were my student friends, all of whom had at least one speciality each. I also discovered that men went into the kitchen quite happily in France, as opposed to the men and boys I knew from the Indian subcontinent who did well to find their way to the kitchen. There was no discrimination between the sexes across the Channel and specifically in the kitchen. Men took pride in cooking and showing off about it. They chose the wine and cheese with awareness. Not surprising really since their fathers had probably done the same thing. I had some of the best meals at homes of young men who opened oysters by the dozen and served perfectly chilled Muscadet along with it. Not very creative but it took a lot of devotion to open a hundred oysters in one evening. The same bunch prepared excellent onion tart, cabbage stuffed with baby pigeon and could select magnificent cheeses.

I was once asked to cook 'Indian' in Paris and concocted something which looked like koftas in a 'Kashmiri' masala gravy. I had found the masala in a grubby Indian grocery-shop near Rue St Denis. It met with great applause but I was too much of a culinary snob to repeat it. I became an excellent cook in everything other than Indian. But more importantly, I learned the meaning of the word 'quality'. I learned how to shop, where to shop, how to avoid supermarkets like the plague, how to pick a perfect Brie, which dressing went with which salad and how to handle a lamb chop. I learned which cut of meat to use for each dish and why the age of the animal was so important to cooking. I was taught well and I was an eager and willing student.

When I returned to university in England, the country had become much more cosmopolitan and wiser in matters of food. The British began drinking wine like they were born to it and were eating quiche like it was their national dish. I approached all this trendy hype with my nose firmly in the air. I was beyond all the fluff. I had lived in Paris. Nothing could better that.

It was decided by majority vote one day that each one in our flat on campus would cook for the rest once a week. I looked through all the fancy recipes I had accumulated and painstakingly written down only to be told that the rest of them wanted me to make a curry. 'A curry?' I thought in disgust. 'Me make curry?' I was appalled. My protests fell on deaf ears. Apparently coq au vin was too elitist. Curry was fine for the proletariat. Instead of calling mother and asking for help, I rushed out and bought a book by a lady called Madhur Jaffrey. Her recipes were immaculately accurate and brought Indian cooking out of the restaurant and into the home. She also gave very convenient alternatives if you didn't have the authentic ingredient. This little paperback became my Bible for the next four years. I turned out fabulous koftas, parathas and baingan ka bhartas. Everyone was amazed and so was I.

I shared a flat with a dancer friend called Jedi. Jedi was originally Sikh. Difficult to believe given his formidable pliés and pas de deux. He was supposed to be studying economics but spent all his waking hours either dancing or cooking. Jedi was a creative cook. He ate like a horse and never put on an ounce. I tasted and put on ten kilos. It was bliss. He was also heavily into health, fitness and nature's own. He now runs a Natural Health Centre and teaches modern dance. So much for the economics! He taught me how to make parathas using only English wholemeal flour and how to make the most delicious palak gosht (mutton in spinach, see recipe later) without a drop of oil. I went beyond my usual repertoire of kheema (mince meat) and masoor dal (orange dal) and began to learn the joys of Punjabi cookery with a healthy twist.

From then on, there was no looking back. I became a fiend with the frying pan. Wherever I travelled, whether it was southern Spain or Russia, Shanghai or Bali, food became my ambassador. It has opened difficult doors and made friendships I will cherish.

I arrived back in Bombay towards 1984 (we had emigrated in 1966) and the rest as they say, is history. I started cooking European food since that is what I missed most and what demanded most applause and experimenting with ingredients available here. I became known professionally as 'the Salad Queen' because of my specialty — salads, each one a different, composite recipe gleaned from my travels and every one presented in a different manner. I looked to Europe for inspiration; especially the sunny countries of the Mediterranean since that is what I knew and what I felt would work well in India. I started experimenting and learning about the Far East, their ingredients and cooking techniques. Finally, I came back to my own backyard and found that this was, as my son puts it, 'where it is all happening.' My strange cross-cultural culinary background has given me the urge and inclination to search for my roots and present them in a palatable but healthier fashion in tune with today's needs.

Many of the recipes in this book are by no means my own. They are recipes I have collected or coerced out of dear friends. Some are almost in their original state. Others have been tried, tested and tampered with. I have relied on the culinary prowess of great friends who cook great food. I grasped the essence of balance, taste and texture of these traditional offerings, spoke to them about how things are served, in what state, to whom, when and why. We talked about seasonal variations and climatic influences and then adapted them both to my tastebuds and to a lighter feel. Here is what I have to say about the people behind my inspiration.

Arunesh Maiyar is a passionate cook. He works in the hospitality industry and is one of the most dedicated teachers I know. He was introduced to usal (sprouts), coconut and peanuts, essential ingredients of his mother's native Maharashtrian food and the satvic simplicity of hashis (raw vegetables and greens) and thumblis (yogurt based coolers) of Karwar in Karnataka, his father's home. He also grew up in Hyderabad with the fire and brimstone of Andhra dishes and the rasams and sambhars of Tamil Nadu. His own distinctive brand of cooking draws from all these experiences, from what he refers to as 'the four neglected cuisines of India,' which are almost oil free in their original form. His range of rasams, bhaths (rice preparations which include curry leaves, lemon, tomato, spinach), raitas (see ladyfinger and mustard raita) and coconut milk curries (see magai kai payday) have faithful and indulgent friends, clamouring for more.

Sumitra Naren is a much sought after landscape designer and another closet cook. Her traditional Maharashtrian and Konkan recipes and slow roasted spices made me realise that we should work together to create some magic. I think we have. We have developed some spice blends for my range of food products known as Lean Cuisine masalas (see Malabar, Kolhapuri, Deccan spice and Sambhar masalas). These spices have been painstakingly roasted and carefully blended so you need no oil at all while cooking.

Many of the recipes in this book owe their origin to my store of friends and family. I thank them all for opening their hearts and homes to me. I reach for **Rebecca Pinto** when I would kill for something unashamedly Goan. Rebecca's recipes are a blend of traditional and easy abbreviations. All of them work well and more important, all of them are very quick. I have adapted them for this book.

I also thank **Ramabai Bakhlé** for her delicious light

recipes for koshimbirs or Maharashtrian salads. She is ninety-one-years old and still sets a splendid table. Ramabai Bakhlé started Pune's first finishing school for Maharashtrian girls. Part of the training included the art of cooking and serving traditional Maharashtrian food including helpful hints and shopping tips which was revolutionary for her time. Her recipes are simple, easy to follow and they work.

My own great aunt, **Marie Wadia** is also ninety-one. She shared some of our secret family recipes with me on condition that I was never to let them out of the family but I couldn't resist sharing our Goan prawn curry with you. It is simply superb. I have managed to repeat it wherever I go in the world with great success and much applause.

There are one or two recipes adapted from traditional ones cooked for me by friends in the profession. These include food columnist **Parvana Boga Noorani** (Parsee recipes), the chefs of culinary impresario **Jiggs Kalra** (Kerela clam and shrimp soup) award winning author, **Gauri Deshpande** (who painstakingly translated from Marathi with her own tips and unforgettable brand of humour) and Executive Chef **Rego** from the Taj, Goa. Rego took me on a tour of Mapuca Market on a wet Sunday afternoon to educate me about Goan fish in the monsoon. **Ismail Merchant's** book on Indian cooking also inspired me. It made me realise that the essence of a great dish lies not in a multitude of ingredients, and hours of preparation but in simple, easy to follow guidelines using ingredients at hand. And I cannot forget to thank **Madhur Jaffrey** who introduced me, through her books, to the variety of Indian regional dishes and aroused enough curiosity in me to pursue this track.

What Lean Cuisine Means

The image of Indian food both here and abroad is generally heavy, rich and spicy. We possess a rich culinary heritage which is not only regarded by connoisseurs as one of the finest in the world, but which much of the world is looking to for inspiration. Somehow, somewhere, things have gone wrong. The gap between the exquisite simplicity of home-made dals, vegetables, fish, meat, salads and raitas and the red, brown and beige slop called 'curries' which we have to suffer in restaurants, is widening.

To be fair, some hotels have started waking up to the idea of a rediscovery of regional cuisines — as long as, of course, they make good commercial sense. But once again, it is the more 'exotic' — succulent kebabs created for toothless nawabs, fragrant biryanis with lacy omelette purdahs and creamy, rich, ghee-laden desserts topped with silver and gold leaf and smothered with all manner of dry fruit — which is pushed. This does nothing to promote the country or its cuisines. Infact, it reinforces the image of India being a land of two extremes — that of the pauper and the maharaja. All those millions of greys in between are again left out. If we were to believe the hospitality industry, south India can only produce the idli and the dosa, north India is responsible for a bright red coloured tandoori and its cousin, the butter chicken and coastal food only consists of fiery coconut curries. Bengal for the most part, doesn't feature at all except for sweetmeats, 'kadhai baby corn mushroom' is actually an Indian dish and vegetarians just want paneer (cottage cheese.)

The current trend worldwide is not a discovery of one's heritage. That has been seen and done and finished with. The trend today, after many slip-ups and much experimentation, is harmony and balance between taste, lightness and tradition.

Cooking techniques are borrowed from the Far East, vegetables remain crisp and colourful, salads invade the menus and fruits reign supreme in the dessert section. Everybody is aware of health and heart attacks and cholesterol is a household word. This does not mean that we have to eat what is known as rabbit food. But we do have to eat with awareness and that awareness has to be part of our everyday lives. Weight loss diets work, but for how long? If your basic lifestyle reverts back to a daily dose of fried food, you have lost the point completely. For my part, I concentrate on recipes using fresh vegetables and spices and in the non-vegetarian section, seafood and white meat. Desserts are often fruit based with the addition of a little alcohol for that extra uplift and chutneys and relishes are light, tangy and oil free.

Let's face it, unless you are a farmer, you are unlikely to be doing the kind of physical exercise which is required to digest many traditional Indian dishes. What most of us want and need are interesting, inspired Indian dishes which are flavoursome, delicious and allow us to breathe comfortably at the end of the meal. Most Indian dishes I eat in restaurants just make me want to collapse in a comfortable chair afterwards!

The collection of lean cuisine recipes I have put together over the years is my answer to this problem. Many recipes, especially those from the south and from the Brahmin Maharashtrian community are pretty lean without my help. They contain very little or no oil at all. The vegetables are steamed with a light tempering or chucked into a thin, sour and peppery liquid. Coconut milk and gravies thickened with grated coconut provide all the essential oils that the body needs. I also firmly believe that the age old practice of frying onions, ginger, garlic, dry spices and meat in oil first until it turns 'golden brown' can be avoided. There are other things you can do to enhance the flavour and make sure that the ingredients are well cooked at the same time, without frying.

I once did a food tasting which lasted a whole week (what indulgence!) where we tried to find out whether wines went with Indian food. We tasted a variety of dishes from all over the country and came to a fairly favourable conclusion. In the process, I put on an uncanny amount of weight despite the fact that I rarely ate more than a fork full of any one dish. I was convinced that it was the oil content in each dish, something that my body is not used to, that did the trick. To be more precise, it is the frying of each ingredient in oil which slows down digestion and makes you put on all that weight. When you fry, you also tend to overcook, which means that you have probably lost any valuable nutritional content in the process too.

Now in the countries of the Mediterranean, olive oil is poured everywhere and the same Michelin tyre effect doesn't happen. Why? Olive oil is predominantly a monounsaturated fat with no cholesterol, which in lay terms means that its cardiovascular benefits make it a healthy choice. The more virgin, or pure the olive oil, the better it is and can be consumed as a raw food without refining or other processing. Raw peanut, sunflower or safflower oil is a good substitute in India. Many of the koshimbirs in this book are traditionally finished off with an oil or ghee tempering. Although I am not personally a fan of ghee and butter, I know many for whom 'tup' (ghee) on rice, chapatis and dal, is sacred. If you can't do without it, don't, but do it in moderation and compensate for it by having an oil free meal later on.

I am not a very meaty person myself, but I have had to come to terms with the fact that both friends and certain members of my family who are almost carnivores, require their daily intake of flesh, be it fish, fowl or beast. The broiler chicken, although convenient, can taste a bit like blotting paper. Mutton, on the other hand, for those who love meat and still want to count their calories, can be a tasty, healthy alternative. Mutton, or rather kid, where I live (in Pune) is slaughtered at around 4 to 6 months old. The meat is pink, lean and succulent and does not require hours of cooking to tenderize it unlike it's counterparts in Bombay. If all the fat is removed from the meat, 100g of mutton contains 13g protein and only 8g fat. It is also an excellent source of niacin, thiamine and iron.

Slow braising or slow cooking both tenderizes meat whilst retaining the flavour. For perfect results, the meat should be marinated for at least a few hours and should not be overcooked until it falls off the bone. I use meat with the bones as this adds flavour and calcium to the dish.

Seafood is definitely the healthier option. It has a very low fat content, is high in protein and fish especially contains valuable omega 3 oils.

If you want to lose some weight quickly, the first thing to do, as we all know, is to start exercising, try and cut out excessive fat, oil and sugar from your diet and stop eating heavy meals late in the evening. This is not difficult on a short term basis. Try and do it for the rest of your life ! I am interested in bringing about a change of lifestyle, which will lead to a healthier, more wholesome life. I am not interested in temporary fads as a solution to a weight problem. Every person is different and nobody has the right to prescribe a diet without knowing your body, your personality, temperament and lifestyle. **Only you can do that**.

I consider oil free cooking just one step in the right direction to a more healthy, vital lifestyle without making too drastic a change too quickly. Believe me, after a while, you won't miss the oil at all!

Something about the Regions Featured in this Book

Goa

Goan cuisine has a casual vivacity that matches its people. It conjures up images of sun-soaked beaches, palm-lined coastlines and paddy fields; pounding waves and nonstop music. Food and fun go as naturally together as fish curry and feni. Although the Portuguese left Goa in 1965, after 451 years of rule, this territory of seven hundred kilometres is still quite distinct from the rest of India. And so is its cuisine. The Portuguese came to India well before the British or even the Moghuls, hence Goan food has developed distinct flavours which rely both on local ingredients like coconut, kokum (a souring agent used in curries), toddy vinegar and plenty of marine life and Portuguese imports from the motherland as well as their other colonies. The chilli was also introduced by the Portuguese to Goa from the New World.

Goan home-style cuisine is a curious blend of Indianised Portuguese, of subtlety and spice. Portuguese specialties like oyster pie, rishois, little puff pastry pasties and guisado de peixe, an oniony fish stew, are enjoyed as much as the pungent Goa sausage, a spicy sister of the Spanish chorizo, and sorpotel, a fiendish stew made with pork and pork offal, cooked in a mountain of spices finely ground in vinegar. Each individual masala or spice paste, is stone ground in traditional Goan cuisine and each is destined to marry, not fight with the other on the table. Today, a mixer, which produces finely ground pastes, will do quite nicely. Coconut is repeated in many preparations, but this does not mean that the flavours produced are similar.

Seafood is a staple for most coastal Goans. Fish and

prawns are dried to make sure that the Goan lust for seafood is satisfied even during the monsoon, when fewer fish are available. Hence, the existence of a whole repertoire of dishes which concentrate on dry fish as a base. Goans eat all manner of seafood, from the fancy lobster and jumbo prawn to the modest clam, ladyfish, crabs, mussels, oysters and fish. They do all sorts of things to fish, but most commonly, fish is coated or stuffed with a red masala, known as ambotik or recheade, and fried. I have used the same masala in the recipes in this book but instead of frying the fish, you can brush with a little oil and grill. Fish is also slipped into velvety smooth coconut curries, which range from mild (caldin) to very spicy.

Karwar

Karwari cuisine (Karwar is on the west coast of India, south of Goa) as practiced by the Havika and Kota Brahmin community is lightness personified. Very little oil is used and that too mainly for seasoning, as coconut has the balance oil needed as nutrients. (Coconut fat is dissolvable fat — hence low on cholesterol, e.g. natural fat and not animal fat.) Ready-made masalas are anathema to traditional Karwari cuisine. All masalas are either roasted in very little oil or blended raw and cooked. Sometimes raw spices are just blended and served unprocessed. The red chilli, long and crinkled, comes from Bedge, a town in Belgaum. It adds a vibrant crimson colour and is not pungent. The same chilli is used in most of my roasted spice blends. Most vegetable curries are steam cooked. The Karwari word for vegetable curries is 'ubkari' or 'steamed vegetables'. Souring agents vary from yogurt, raw mango, lime, and tamarind to kokum, and bimbli kai as it is everywhere on the Konkan coast and are designed to combat the heat. Remember, never over boil coconut curries as the oil will separate and alter the taste and the texture of the final product.

Uncommon vegetables used often in Karwari cuisine

- raw banana
- raw jackfruit and jackfruit seeds
- banana flowers
- banana stems
- fresh arrowroot
- sweet potatoes
- pineapple fruit as a savoury ingredient
- bamboo shoots
- lemon grass
- karambol / star fruit
- hog — plum-green mango lookalike
- magai — Madras cucumber (large green/yellow, like a pumpkin)

All the gravy dishes should be eaten with slightly sticky or wet rice. Unpolished rice enhances the flavour even more.

Maharashtra

Maharashtrian cuisine is one of the lesser known cuisines of India. Like many other cuisines of India, it suffers because there is very little written down. It has not been actively promoted or hyped either, perhaps because it lacks glamour and sophistication. Generally speaking Maharashtrians are regarded as quietly understated people who are not prone to fuss, pampering or excess. Their food follows similar patterns and therefore adapts itself very well to lean cuisine.

When you are invited to a Maharashtrian home, even the most sophisticated one, you will get home food. Nothing will be bought and it will more than likely be a very traditional meal without borrowing from any foreign cuisines or even other regions of India. You may have, for example, usal (sprouts) or valache birda (split white beans which have a bitter aftertaste) or a main vegetable dish of eggplant (bharli wangi), a leafy vegetable, simple salad of grated vegetables, (koshimbir), yogurt, bhaakri (hand flattened roti made with millet or sorghum) and kadhi or dal and rice. If the family eats meat, then a chicken or mutton dish may appear. Chicken is usually cut into small pieces through the bone and not at the joints. There may be a sweet dish if there is a special occasion, rotis stuffed with a mixture of jaggery and chickpea flour known as puran poli or a simple shrikhand. In between meals, you can snack on flaky biscuits known as chirothas and during the festival of Ganpati, you are likely to find sweet steamed dumplings called modaks as part of a vegetarian meal.

The meal itself is a refreshing change and is almost spiritual in its simplicity. This does not mean, however, that the dishes are either easy to prepare or that they have been thrown together in some ad hoc fashion. Many of them require a deft hand, are time consuming and take years of experience to get just right. And much planning goes into what to combine together in taste, texture and visual appeal. If there is one spicy masala preparation then it will be complimented by a simple, steamed vegetable with a light tempering. Sweets are not a necessary part of the meal. It is the details which one has to look out for in Maharashtrian food, not the overall impression.

Living in Pune, I have had the fortune of being exposed to the four very distinct regional varieties within this state. Konkan Maharashtrian food is divided into the coastal belt and inland. The community from the coast are made up of Brahmin vegetarians whose dishes are coconut based, using little or no spice in the form of garlic, ginger and red chilli. They concentrate on simple temperings of green chilli and curry leaves and specialise in dishes using the banana flower, stem and fruit, tapioca and rice bhaakri and rice as a staple. These Brahmins have light eyes and fair complexions, the origin of which is unclear but is often attributed to Greek traders who hit the coast. Karwaris and Saraswats included fish in their diet but again, the emphasis is on simple preparations using less spice. Further inland, the Konkans use peanut, sesame and coriander as spicing agents and eat sorghum bhaakri.

Kolhapur, in central Maharashtra heading south to Belgaum is home to the richer, more spicy dishes of the state. Kolhapur was home to the Marathas who were the ruling dynasty and hence the dishes concentrated on meat both in dry dishes as well as curries like the famous Kolhapuri mutton using a spice blend made originally from over 20 individual ingredients. By spices I refer to cinnamon, clove, cardamom, black pepper, mace and so on and not to chilli. Concentrated goat blood known as rakti is added to meat dishes for flavour and game meat is very popular in the Kolhapur Satara traditional hunting belt. The chilli belt begins towards Belgaum and proceeds south into Karnataka.

Lastly, Vidarbha food from the north of the state around Nagpur and Jalgaon concentrates on simple preparations with fiery hot, oily temperings of chilli and garlic, mouth burning chilli and garlic concoctions known as tetcha and down to earth, hearty dishes like their famous baingan ka bhartha (eggplant) tempered with roasted chilli paste.

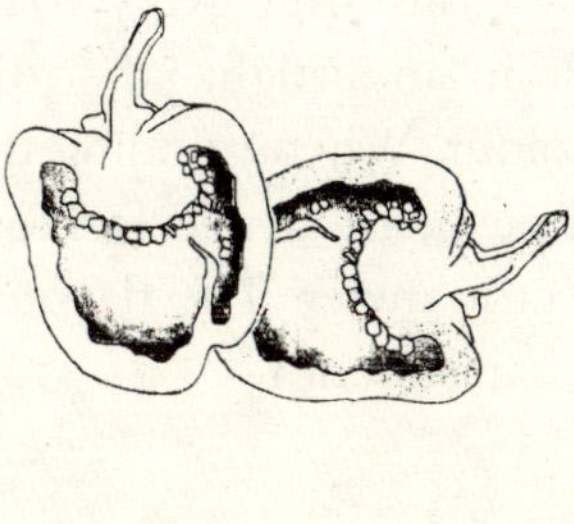

How to Change Your Lifestyle into an Oil Free One

You don't have to turn your kitchen upside down for oil free cooking. In fact it is a much more simple and faster process than ordinary cooking with oil. You need no special equipment, no fancy sauces nor a fantastic budget. Lean cuisine dishes can be made from everyday ingredients in your normal utensils. What you will need to do is practice and master the following:

Roasting

Roasting is essential to oil free cooking. The spices you would have fried in order to cook them and get a colour can be dry roasted like peanuts instead. I personally find the flavour of roasted spices superior to fried ones. To roast you will need a tawa or a heavy, preferably cast iron, frying pan. It helps if the tawa is seasoned and black with wear and tear. A wooden spatula is also helpful. A tawa is actually ideal as it is cheap and available all over the country. Heat the tawa first. When it is very hot, add the spices one by one until the colour slightly changes and a wonderful aroma fills your kitchen. If it looks like the spices are turning to cinders, remove the tawa from the fire immediately, remove the spices, wipe the tawa with a clean, dry cloth and continue on a lower heat. It might be a good idea to wipe your tawa or pan with a dry cloth after every roasting of individual spices. Keep these in an airtight jar so that they don't lose their flavour or colour. When grinding these spices, try and use a mortar and pestle or an old-fashioned grinding stone rather than an electric mixer. The flavour and colour in the hand methods is far superior.

Roasting onion and garlic is another way to maintain flavour without oil. Place the onions and garlic whole (do not peel) in a roasting pan. You can brush them with a little oil to prevent sticking. Always keep a basting brush (or fat paint brush which you only use for basting!) handy. Place the pan or tray in a moderately hot oven. If you are roasting large quantities, roast the onions and garlic separately, or else one will be burnt when the other is just done. 1 kg onions take approximately 1 to 1½ hours depending upon the size of the onions. Remove, cool, peel the outer crispy layer only and chop before adding to any dish in place of fried onions. Garlic can be peeled and chopped or made into a paste. Roasted onions and garlic can be refrigerated for upto ten days without any risk of spoilage. They form the base for most gravy dishes, soups and pullaos. Whenever you read 'fry the onions until golden' in other cookery books, replace with equal amounts of roasted ones.

Steaming

For this you will need a steamer or simply a stainless steel sieve, which sits comfortably inside a handi or saucepan, which can be removed easily and has a tight fitting lid. Both are easily available. Heat water in the handi or outer pan of the steamer. You do not need to add litres of water. You are steaming, not boiling. The more water you add, the longer the whole process will take. For ½ kg vegetable, you will need no more than 3 cups of water. To the water you can add lemon juice, garlic, onions and herbs. This will impart a delicate flavour to whatever you are steaming. When the water begins to boil steadily, put your vegetables in the sieve and shut the lid tight. The process of steaming is very quick. You will have to do it a few times to judge cooking times for yourself. The crunchier the vegetables, the more healthy they are and the more vibrant they look.

For certain dishes which require steaming with tempered

spices, you will need an old fashioned kadhai or wok with a tight lid and a separate cast iron, well seasoned tempering ladle or small frying pan.

Slow Cooking

This is essential in the preparation of meat and gravy dishes. You will need plenty of liquid, a tightly fitting lid and a heavy-bottomed handi or pan. The French cast iron set known as Le Creuset is ideal, so are old brass and copper woks which have a good inner metal coating (calhai). Coconut curries are delicious when cooked traditionally in earthenware pots over coal or wood fires. You can also use them directly on the gas provided you use a constant low flame. You can also slow cook in the oven. I am not a fan of pressure cookers. I can never judge cooking times and amounts of liquid properly and I always, and invariably overcook everything in them. If, however, you know your instrument well and can cope with faulty whistles and temperature gauges, go ahead. Nonetheless, I still maintain that food slow cooked the traditional way tastes much, much better.

Making Stock

A good vegetable, onion or chicken stock is essential to oil free cooking. Your ingredients will cook in a flavoursome cooking medium without fat. Make a pot of stock and keep it in the fridge. Vegetable and onion stock will last for a week easily. Chicken or meat stock should be cooled, skimmed of all fat and then refrigerated. For onion stock, slice 6 onions, put them in a pan with 15 cups of water, some peppercorns, a bay leaf or two and a couple of cloves. Boil and then simmer until the onions are very soft and the liquid has reduced by half. Use as is or strain.

Brown Rice

Brown rice can be boring. It can also be tough (very hard work for the jaws), pretty tasteless and mushy. However, since it is so healthy and nutritious, being an excellent source of niacin, magnesium and iron and a moderate source of protein, fibre and zinc, we really should be eating more of it. As part of a high energy, low fat diet, there is nothing better. The bran layer of rice, which includes the embryo of the seed (which is removed during the milling of white rice) gives brown rice a superior vitamin content. Try also to cook the rice in the exact amount of water needed in order to avoid losing those valuable vitamins.

For rice salad, remember not to overcook the rice to a gruel like consistency. It should be chewy but not tough. After the rice is cooked, turn it out onto a flat dish to cool. Brown rice is available in all health stores and some supermarkets in Bombay. In Pune, ABC Farms who have outlets on MG Road, Shivaji Market and Kondhwa, produce an excellent long grain variety which looks like American wild rice and is grown organically on their farm. Anyone visiting Goa should try and get hold of unpolished red rice (local rice) which is both tasty, nutritious and available at local markets in Mapusa, Panaji and Margaon. The Goans make a delicious morning porridge from it.

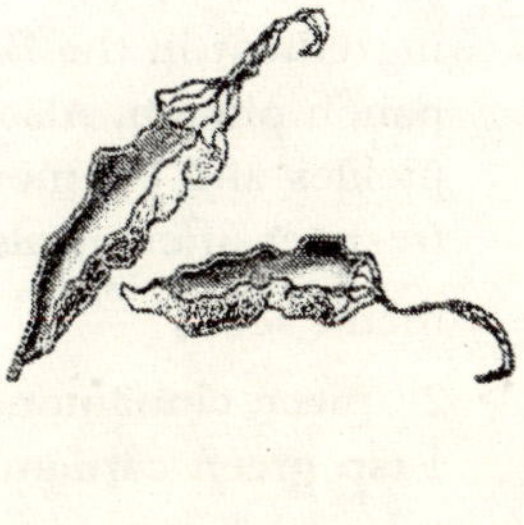

Ingredients Used in This Book

asafoetida	hing (powder), never use more than a pinch. It is used a great deal in Maharashtrian cooking
bay leaf	tej patta
black or rock salt	kala namak. Light purple in colour. Essential in all north Indian snacks and chaats
cardamom	elaichi, green or black. Can be used whole or remove casing and grind seeds to a powder form
chaat masala	½ tbsp dry mango powder, ½ tsp black salt, 1 tbsp black pepper, 1 tbsp roasted cumin seeds, a pinch of asafoetida and dry ginger powder
cinnamon	dalchini. Usually sold in bark form or powdered
cloves	lavang
curry leaf	kadi patta
dry ginger powder	sonth. Used widely in Kashmiri cooking and chaats
dry mango powder	amchur, a sweet sour powder of dried raw mangoes. Used in north Indian dishes, on grilled meats and essential to chaat and consequently chaat masala
fennel /aniseed seeds	sonf. Used a great deal in Kashmiri dishes alongwith dry ginger powder. It is also an essential ingredient in the Bengali spice mix, panch phoran. Also used widely in pickles and chutneys, as a mouth freshner after meals and a digestive
fenugreek seeds	methi seeds
garam masala	2" piece cinnamon, 1 tsp cloves, 1 tsp green cardamom (seeds only),

	1 black cardamom (seeds only), 1 tsp black pepper, ½ tsp nutmeg, 1 bay leaf
millet	bajra
nigella or onion seeds	kalonji
peanut powder	moongphali, ground finely. Can be done at home or bought readymade.
pepper (corns)	kali mirch powder (whole)
rice flour	chawal ka atta, made by soaking, drying and grinding rice. Also available ready-made
sesame seeds	til
sorghum	jovar
turmeric	haldi
white poppy seeds	khus khus
whole cumin seeds	jeera
whole mustard seeds	rai, (black, brown/red or split yellow)

Pulses/Vegetables etc.

aubergine/eggplant	baigan
blackeyed beans	chowli
brown/black/ green chickpeas	kabuli channa. Green can be used fresh. Just steam for a few minutes or eat fresh from the pod
chickpea dal	channa dal
coriander	fresh, green dhania
cottage cheese	paneer made with full cream milk
cream	malai
dry flattened rice	poha, also eaten as a breakfast cereal and used widely in vegetarian dishes in Maharashtra
fenugreek	fresh green methi. Sold in bunches with small green leaves. In Mumbai, 'choto methi' or small leaf fenugreek which looks like English cress is available in most markets, especially in winter. It

	is grown in sand and along the sides of the railway tracks and therefore is particular to this city. It has a milder flavour than its cousin and is also excellent in raw salads
halwa	semolina cooked in milk and garnished with raisins and nuts
hung curd	chakka
jaggery	gur or unrefined cane sugar
kheema	mince meat
kidney beans	rajma (pink or maroon/brown)
kofta	dumplings
kokum	black outer casing of a fruit. Used as a souring agent in Goan dishes
lime	limboo, but also referred to as lemon
mace	javitri
mint	pudina
nutmeg	jaiphal
orange dal	masoor dal. Whole masoor is dark brown and needs soaking
parathas	stuffed rotis
plain white flour	maida
pomegranate	anaar
puris	puffed fried flour rotis
soya/dil	shepu
tamarind	imli, available in fresh, dry and pulp form
white dal	urad dal, is used a lot in south Indian preparations
yellow dal	moong dal, which is probably the most simple dal to cook. Whole moong is green, which needs soaking and is also excellent for sprouts
yellow split dal	tuar dal

Lean Cuisine Ingredients

Carrots

I once bought some carrots from a store in Pune, which were by far the tastiest, juiciest ones I had tasted for some time. They were small, the largest was maybe six inches long, with an attractive cluster of delicate ferny green leaves and came, I believe, from Mahabaleshwar. What are commonly known as 'English' carrots in India, is a bit of a fallacy. They are bright orange for sure, but often much tougher and quite tasteless compared to the 'desi' or dark orange, slightly hairy Indian variety. Carrots are root vegetables which are high in potassium, carotene or vitamin A and a good deal of vitamin C. They contain almost no fat but a good amount of dietary fibre. 100g of carrots (approximately 1 cup grated raw) contains only 23 calories.

Carrots were included in the list of medical plants by the Greeks and Romans. They were not used as food in Europe until the fourteenth century and the feathery green leaves were worn as decoration both in Holland and in the court of Charles I!

Carrots should be washed in cold water, brushed or peeled very thinly before boiling or steaming. They are crunchy and slightly sweet, so are perfect for salads, as sticks for dips and sweet dishes like carrot halwa or carrot cake.

Melons

Summer is the ideal time to shed those unwanted kilos by going on a fruit-based diet. We, in India, are extremely lucky to have such a large variety of delicious, sweet fruit. Melon is the perfect fruit for the heat and like fruits such as pineapple and grapes are diuretic, which means that they can actually help you lose weight too. However, be warned, although many people do go on a diet of grapes only, primarily to detoxify the body, this should not be done with melon.

Until now in India we have had watermelons and mash melons. They are large and have a corky, nettled surface on a golden brown skin and are fragrant with a slightly soft, sweet orange flesh. I have recently noticed the honeydew variety in Bombay. This is medium sized, oval and has a thick, clear, yellow skin with crispy, pale green flesh. It is both fragrant as well as extremely sweet. Although honeydew is a native of Asia, it is today cultivated in the Middle East, southern Europe, Australia and America. The Israelis grow an even better variety called ogen. Charentais also called cavaillon, with a hard pale green skin with dark green ribs and deep golden orange flesh, is the French favourite. Of the rock melon varieties (those with scaly, yellow green skin which are from Central Asia originally), we sometimes see one resembling a cantaloupe, small and round with yellow orange flesh. These are available all over Delhi and north India in summer. Recently, deliciously sweet, dark yellow melons with crisp green flesh, have been flooding the markets.

Choosing a melon can prove problematic. I have seen people press, shake and smell these fruit in a desperate attempt to find a sweet one. I spent several summers in the south of France as a teenager watching old men in berets take a melon in the palm of their hand (to choose a heavy fruit which is full of flesh as opposed to a light, airy one), press the top gently with their thumb (if it just yields, then it is ripe) and finally smell it. If the fruit smells fragrant, it is bound to be sweet. If the fruit is ripe when you buy it and you are not going to consume it immediately, put it in the fridge. In any case, melon is best served chilled. Melon is also an excellent source of vitamin C and iron.

Melons can be cut up, discarding the seeds and outer skin, and eaten in slices or chopped in a fruit salad. The French scoop out the seeds of small cavaillon melons, and fill them with port or serve them in slices with prosciutto or parma ham as a starter. You can also sprinkle them with powdered ginger as a fruit course, cut it into balls with a melon ball scoop or puree it for use in drinks, ice cream and soups!

Onions and Tomatoes

Remember that a chopped tomato or onion in any dish will prevent the vegetables or meat from sticking to the pan and will also give you a fairly neutral cooking base. If you cook the onions and tomatoes enough, you probably won't even know that they have been added at all. Make sure that you blanch the tomatoes in hot water first. This will make removing the skins much quicker and easier. Remove the dark notch where they were attached to their stems and chop. If there are too many seeds, then remove and discard them.

Yogurt

In lean cuisine recipes, you will see 'whisked, whipped, blended or beaten yogurt', mentioned quite often. Although yogurt (curds, dahi) is nutritionally similar to milk, it has properties which assist in restoring any imbalance of the healthy organisms in the stomach. Yogurt is also much easier to digest than milk. Fermenting of milk to make yogurt provides a safe substance particularly in our hot climates. Whipping, whisking or blending must be done with a balloon or hand whisk. Treat this as an essential part of your kitchen equipment, not a little fancy add on. With a balloon whisk, watery or lumpy yogurt is transformed to the consistency of cream in seconds. It is then easier to add into raitas, salads and gravies. Always add yogurt a little at a time to a hot dish. Never add to boiling liquid, as it will curdle. Use fresh yogurt, not some that has been lying around for days. The nutritional properties will not change, but it will be very sour and change the flavour of your dish.

Tamarind Paste

Prepare tamarind paste by immersing tamarind in warm water for 10 minutes. Strain through a fine sieve. Alternatively, tamarind paste is also available in most general stores.

Ginger/Garlic Pastes

Make these by peeling the ginger and garlic and running it through a blender with a little water. Alternatively, ready-made pastes are available. Watch out for the salt content in these pastes!

Sauces

Sauces and gravies are traditionally thickened by frying onions in plenty of oil and then slow cooking. With lean cuisine recipes, the same ingredients are just slow cooked in water or stock and the sauce is reduced considerably. What you end up with is tasty gravy, which has been thickened without the use of flour or frying in oil. The only snag is in the case of gravies. You sometimes have to reduce them (can be time consuming) so that the masala sticks onto the fish or meat. Since there is no oil, you must stir constantly to prevent sticking.

Meat, Fish and Fowl

All meat and chicken should be trimmed of all fat. It goes without saying that chicken skin has to be removed for lean cuisine recipes. Fish skin is not fattening or oily, and can be left on, especially when grilling.

A Note on Pulses

Dal recipes are probably the easiest Indian ones to convert to 'lean cuisine'. On the whole, dals are healthy because they are an excellent source of protein, fibre and the B vitamins. If you are used to a tadka or tempering, just replace with roasted spices. Instead of frying onion, ginger or garlic, cook them in stock to soften them or cook them directly in the dal. The latter is especially possible with whole dals, chickpeas and beans (rajma, chowli) which take ages to cook anyway. Remember that you must always soak whole beans (chickpea, kidney beans, split peas, and whole dals) overnight. Rinse in several changes of water before cooking.

Garlic

Garlic in India varies in pungency according to the season. Young or new garlic is tender and less pungent than dry pods. 3 cloves of Indian garlic is roughly equivalent to 1 clove of Spanish or Italian.

Chillies

Green chillies always refer to fresh green chillies available in all markets in India. They vary in size, shape and shades of green. They also range from the mild to the very hot. Choose according to your taste buds.

Red chillies refer in most cases to Kashmiri or Bedge, (pronounced Bed-gé) which are dry, red chillies. They have a great deal of colour and are easy on the spice. For use in masala pastes, remove the stalk and soak in water for 10-15 minutes. Drain the water and any loose seeds and grind. Always remove the stalk even when roasting directly on the tawa or griddle.

Red chilli powder is readily available but its origins and pungency are unreliable. Always taste chilli powder before you use it.

Good Vegetable Stock

This can also be eaten as a soup (it is actually a diuretic), hot or cold. The trick is not to overcook the vegetables.

Ingredients

2 large tomatoes, blanched, peeled and chopped

2 large green capsicums, de-seeded and chopped
1 cup celery, chopped fine
2 onions, sliced thin
Salt to taste (you actually need very little since the celery contains a whole lot of natural salt)
7½ cups water

Method

Remember to clean the celery well before chopping. Indian celery is full of flavour but tends to be very stringy so you must always chop it fine. Add all the above ingredients to a pan with the water. Boil and simmer until the veggies are just cooked. Add salt if needed. Serve as a soup or strain and use as a basic vegetable stock.

Wholegrain Mustard

Ingredients
3½ cups black mustard seeds
1 tsp salt
2 tsp sugar
7½ cups vinegar

Method

Soak the black mustard seeds in vinegar overnight. They will have absorbed most of the liquid by the morning. Next day, run it through a blender with the sugar and salt until mixed thoroughly. The texture should be coarse. Bottle and refrigerate.

Souring Agents

Tamarind, tomatoes, kokum, lemon juice and vinegar are often used in lean cuisine recipes for added punch and flavour. You should ideally only use sugarcane or good malt vinegar. Sugarcane vinegar is manufactured by Kolah's in Navsari and is sold in packets and bottles. Malt vinegar is available in bottles. Imported cider or white wine vineger is good for salads and whole grain mustard.

Roasted Spice Blends

Each ingredient must be individually roasted on a tawa, cast iron griddle or heavy frying pan until its colour changes and it emits a smoky, full aroma. Then hand pound (ideally) or grind altogether in a coffee grinder to a fine powder. The method for the Sambhar, Kolhapuri, Malabar and Deccan spice is the same.

Sambhar Masala

This can be used for traditional south Indian sambhar, rasam or any south Indian style vegetarian dish.

Ingredients

7-8 dry red chillies (preferably Bedge or Kashmiri varieties)
2 tsp coriander seeds
1 tsp black pepper
½ tsp turmeric
1 tsp yellow split dal
1 tsp chickpea dal
½ tsp black mustard seeds
½ tsp cumin seeds

Kolhapuri Masala

This is an abbreviated version of the original masala from Kolhapur, which has over 20 ingredients. I have purposely omitted some of them, as they are very difficult to find outside Maharashtra. However, this spice blend still retains the essence and all the flavour and pungency necessary for those fiery Deccan dishes. This is, of course, essential to Kolhapuri mutton but is equally good with brinjal, mixed vegetables and brinjal with dry prawns, which is made in villages in Maharashtra.

Ingredients

12 cloves
2" piece cinnamon
½ tsp black pepper
1 full piece mace
1 tsp coriander seeds
1 bayleaf
2 tsp khus khus
¼ tsp cumin seeds
½ tsp fennel seeds
1 piece star-anise
1 cardamom (skin removed)
7-8 dry red chillies (preferabley Bedge or Kashmiri)

Malabar Masala

I call this Malabar Magic because all you need is a teaspoon or so, a little lemon juice and salt to liven up any seafood. Try it as a marinade for crab, clams, prawns and fish and even in a curry.

Ingredients

10 dry red chillies (preferably Bedge or Kashmiri)
1 tsp coriander seeds
1 tsp black pepper
½ tsp black mustard seeds
a pinch of nutmeg

6 cloves
2" cinnamon
a pinch of asafoetida
½ tsp turmeric

Deccan Spice

In Maharashtra this is known as goda masala. It is used widely to flavour dals, pullaos and thrown liberally into a wok of cooked vegetables. Every house used to make their own goda masala but this is becoming more and more rare since these spices need to be really slow roasted individually which is highly time consuming.

Ingredients
4 tsp coriander seed
1½ tsp sesame seeds
1 tsp cumin seeds
a pinch of asafoetida
¼ tsp turmeric
4 cloves
2" piece cinnamon
1 cardamom (skin removed)
a pinch of grated nutmeg
½ tsp salt
2 tsp desiccated coconut

Ambotik Spice Paste

Every household in Goa, however humble, has a big jar of ambotik or sour-hot masala sitting in the kitchen. It looks very red; the colour coming from the generous use of Kashmiri chilli which when reconstituted in water releases more colour than spice. Vinegar helps it to last. Traditionally, toddy vinegar is used to grind all masalas in Goa. You can substitute toddy vinegar with sugarcane or good malt vinegar. Ambotik is also known in Goa as recheade which comes from the Portuguese 'recheado', meaning 'stuff', and while the paste is mainly used to stuff local fish, it is also used to curry squid and other creatures of the sea and forms the basis of balchao and vindaloo dishes.

What is not used should be put in a jar, covered and refrigerated. It will keep for months.

Ingredients

15 dry red Kashmiri chillies
½ tsp cumin seeds
5 cloves
1" piece cinnamon
1 tsp black pepper
2" piece ginger
1 tsp salt
10 cloves garlic
½ cup malt vinegar

Method

Grind all the above to a fine paste with vinegar.

The Secret of a Good Steak in India

There is never a sure shot guarantee or a completely satisfactory recipe for successful tender steaks. Abroad, steaks are often tender not because of hours of careful marination or clever butchers, but simply because the meat is injected with a great many hormones, massaged while still in its live form (Kobe) or marbled with fat. Meat is also hung up in a cold room after it is slaughtered. This ensures some degree of tenderness as the muscles are allowed to firm up and the blood can drain out. In India, our meat does not go through all these processes and neither is it hung, simply because we do not have cold rooms. It is slaughtered, transported, cut up, sold and cooked like a chain link.

When I first came back to India, I was told that good steak was impossible to find. And certainly what I had tasted in clubs and some restaurants, confirmed that. The steaks were bashed to smithereens; they were usually tough and smothered with an inordinate amount of Worcestershire sauce. On a trip to Delhi one winter, I ordered a medium rare steak from room service at the Taj, Mansingh Road where I was staying. I gave no specific instructions except that I didn't want it 'bashed'. The steak was perfection: juicy, perfectly cooked and melted in the mouth. It was accompanied by creamy mashed potatoes and spinach bundles, which had been blanched and then tossed in a little garlic butter. This is what good food is all about — memories. And I still remember the steak of the winter of 1984 because it was so perfect and so unexpected.

A few days later, I had a similar experience with a filet of beef tenderloin at the house of a French friend in Delhi, Phillipe Lenglet. Phillipe is an extraordinary cook himself and so I asked him whether there was something special about the beef in Delhi or did he share his butcher with the Taj or was it simply a happy coincidence? He firstly advised me that it was only worth buying what is known as 'undercut' in India. This is the lean, boneless piece, which lies below the ribs and is almost always very tender. Other cuts of beef, in India anyway, are a risky proposition, unlike the U.S and Europe. Do not cut the filet of the undercut right away. Phillipe's advice was to freeze it for at least 2 days. Then defrost (not completely, as it is easier to cut meat when it is a little frozen). Clean, trim and cut into steaks crosswise, against the grain, into 1" thick slices.

For roast beef or a whole filet of tenderloin, marinate at room temperature with a little olive oil, salt, pepper and garlic (herbs and spices are optional) for upto an hour or in a fridge overnight. When you fry or grill steaks, the temperature must be very high so that your meat is seared on both sides and does not let out those precious juices. The same applies to a roast. Preheat your oven and then place your roast in the centre of the oven. Turn once while cooking. Alternatively, you can wrap the roast in foil and half cook it with the foil wrapped and then open the foil towards the end of cooking. This method will give you more steak juices to play around with later if you want to make a sauce. The same method can be used for roast chicken (without skin). Wrap the whole chicken in foil with all your herbs, spices and a little salt. I like to use plenty of celery with chicken. It has a lovely flavour and contains natural salt so you don't need a lot of extra white salt.

If you like your meat really well done but still juicy, choose a recipe which entails slow cooking or braising. With mutton, try to buy young goat (kid), which is pink. There is nothing worse (or more chewy) than an old goat! Go for small chops, double or single, expertly cut by a good butcher.

Pork needs no advice, make sure your supplier is reliable and that the meat is cooked to submission.

Fishy Facts

Fish is a nutritional gold mine rich in vitamins and heart protein omega 3 oils, which have been found to reduce the risk of blood clotting and possible inflammation in conditions such as arthritis. Fish and seafood are an excellent source of protein and especially those caught in tropical waters such as ours, have a very low fat content (0.5-2%). Even these fats are rich in polyunsaturated fatty acids. Seafood is the best food source of iodine and fluoride.

Crustaceans and mollusks which are plentiful in the rains are good sources of calcium especially those edible bones such as dried Bombay duck. Crabs and oysters are excellent sources of zinc. Seafood in general is an excellent source of b12, b6, thiamine, and riboflavin.

It is a myth that shellfish are cholesterol builders and bad for your heart. Although some shellfish, such as squid and prawns are high, others that feed on microplant life are actually quite low on cholesterol, about 30 mg in 3.5 ounces of mussels, scallops and clams, and about 55 mg in oysters. Most importantly, they are very low in total fat and unsaturated fat. High fat sauces and mayonnaise can hurt your heart more than a portion of clam and lobster.

Crustaceans: They have an external skeleton, which sometimes forms a fragile jointed shell, e.g. prawns, crab, lobsters, crayfish, scampi.

Mollusks: They are vertebrates protected by a strong shell and are estuary or shore dwelling, e.g. squid, oysters, mussels, scallops, clams, cuttlefish, octopus.

Cooking Techniques and Shortcuts

How to buy, open and prepare a coconut

Before buying a coconut, shake it to make sure it is full of water. The fresher the coconut the more liquid it will have, so select one that is comparatively heavy for its size. (Coconut without liquid and with moldy or wet 'eyes' is likely to be unfit for use).

How to open a coconut

Heat the oven to 250°C. Puncture two of the three smooth dark eyes of the coconut by hammering the tip of an ice pick or a screwdriver through them. Drain off all the coconut liquid into a measuring cup if you plan to use it.

Bake the empty coconut for 15 minutes, then transfer it to a chopping board. While the coconut is still hot, split the shell with a sharp blow of a hammer. The shell should fall away from the coconut. If bits of flesh still cling to the shell, cut them away with a small knife.

How to grate a coconut

Pare off the brown outer skin of the coconut flesh with a swivel-type peeler or a small, sharp knife. Then grate the flesh piece by piece with a hand grater. The tediousness of grating coconut can also be lessened by soaking a whole coconut in warm water for 2 minutes and cracking it into two equal halves — and then prized out by a knife and grating it on a grater, blender or dry grinder.

How to make coconut milk

Cut or break the white of the coconut into 1" pieces. Preferably remove the brown skin and place in the jar of an electric blender. Grind the coconut until it forms a grated mess. Add hot, but not boiling water, cover the jar, and blend at high speed. Strain through a sieve. This is the first milk, which should be the consistency of thin cream. For the second, or thin milk, put the coconut back into the blender with hot water and repeat the process.

Coconut milk spoils very quickly. Refrigerate or use immediately. There is no substitute for grated coconut. Unsweetened desiccated coconut reconstituted in warm water is acceptable if you are desperate but is not as good. However, very good quality coconut cream and milk is widely available in tetra packs under the brand 'Coco Chef'. Nestle's dehydrated coconut powder which can be reconstituted with water and canned coconut milk are also very good substitutes to fresh coconut milk.

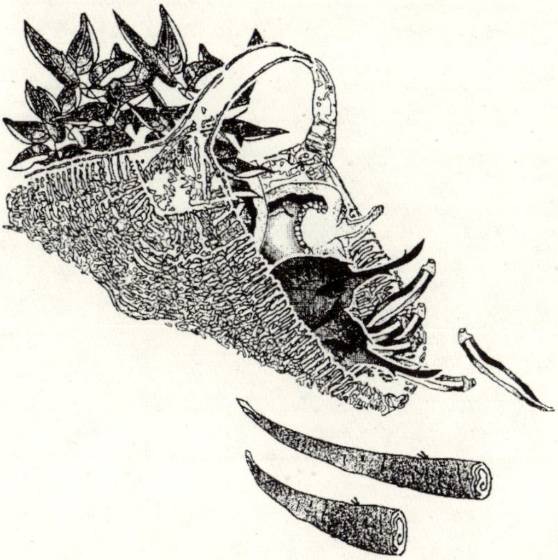

Soups & Starters

North India

Pineapple and Cottage Cheese Chaat

Serves 4

Ingredients

1 fresh pineapple
2 tsp chaat masala
1 tbsp honey
½ cup mint chopped fine (keep aside a few sprigs for garnishing before chopping)
200g cottage cheese cut into ½" cubes

Method

Cut pineapple lengthwise, keeping the green tuft intact, and carefully scoop out the flesh from both sides with a sharp knife. Discard the core and chop remaining pineapple into ½" cubes. Toss the pineapple in a bowl with the chaat masala, honey, mint and cottage cheese.

Serve in the pineapple shell and garnish with sprigs of fresh mint. If chaat masala is not available, replace with a mixture of black salt, a pinch of asafoetida, a pinch of dry ginger powder, dry mango powder and roasted cumin. If your pineapple is not very sweet, then increase the quantity of honey.

Spinach with Yogurt and Walnuts

Serves 4

Ingredients

3½ cups yogurt, whipped lightly

½ tsp garlic paste

salt to taste

1 tbsp honey

3-4 bunches/700g fresh spinach, washed in several changes of water (never squeeze water out of raw spinach as the leaves will darken where they have torn)

1 tsp fresh coarsely ground black pepper

½ cup walnuts, finely chopped and some larger pieces for garnish

Method

Mix the garlic, salt to taste and honey into the yogurt. Steam or blanch the spinach in batches until it just wilts. Cool. Drain and squeeze out all the excess water. Chop roughly. Add spinach and the fresh ground pepper to the yogurt mixture and mix well. Stir in the chopped walnuts. Garnish with larger pieces of walnuts before serving.

Chill and serve as a salad or as a raita. You can also serve this as a dip. Buy a round, crusty loaf of bread. Carefully scoop out the centre, taking care not to touch the bottom and fill it with the dip. After all the dip is over, you can eat the bread which has by then soaked up some of the dip!

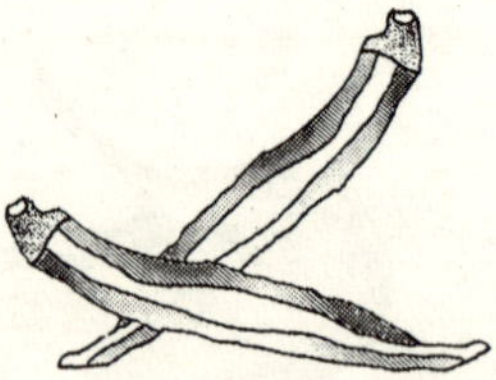

Beetroot with Zing

Serves 4

Ingredients

4 medium sized beetroots
2 tbsp onions, chopped fine
1 tbsp celery, chopped fine
1 tbsp whole grain mustard
1 cup yogurt, lightly whipped
1 small, raw mango, chopped fine (optional)
salt to taste
¼ tsp red chilli powder or a generous dash of Tabasco

Method

Boil the beetroots whole with their skins until tender. Cool completely. Cut into 1" cubes. Mix all the remaining ingredients in a bowl. Add the beetroot. Mix well. The bowl would look pretty messy by now, so transfer to a clean bowl to serve. Serve at room temperature. If you chill this salad, the yogurt tends to become dry around the edges of the bowl. Serve with onion rings.

Potato and Mustard Salad

Serves 2

Ingredients

2 cups potatoes, boiled and cut into 1" cubes
½ cup yogurt, whisked until smooth
½ cup hung curd
1 tbsp ginger, finely sliced and soaked in ½ tbsp lime juice
2 tbsp fresh coriander, finely chopped
1 tsp salt

Blend to a fine paste with a little water the following
1 tsp whole grain mustard
2 dry red chilli
½ tsp cumin
2 tbsp fresh coconut

Method

Cut the potatoes into cubes while they are still warm. Mix in the spice paste and salt. Stir well and leave to marinate for at least ½ hour. Whisk the yogurt and the hung curd until smooth. Add to the potatoes along with the ginger, and coriander. Serve at room temperature.

N.B. If the yogurt or hung curd is a little sour, add a teaspoon of honey to it while whisking.

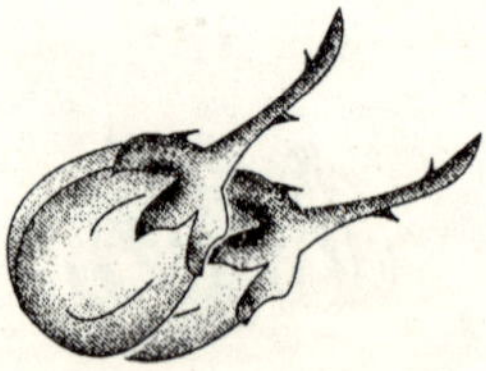

Mustard & Orange Salad

Serves 4

Ingredients

6 oranges

½ tsp salt

1 tsp sugar

2 tbsp lime juice

1 tsp red mustard seeds slightly crushed in a mortar and pestle

Blend until smooth with 1 tbsp of water the following

1 dried red chilli, soaked and de-seeded

¼ tsp cumin seeds

2 tbsp fresh coconut

Method

Peel the oranges and divide into segments removing the skin of each segment. (This is laborious but worth it). Add the masala paste. Mix thoroughly. Add salt, sugar and lime juice and crushed mustard seeds. Toss, chill and serve.

You can replace the orange with 1 whole pineapple (cut and cubed into 1" pieces) or cucumber (peeled, cored and cut into 1" pieces).

If using cucumber add a few roasted curry leaves and ½ teaspoon roasted black mustard as garnish.

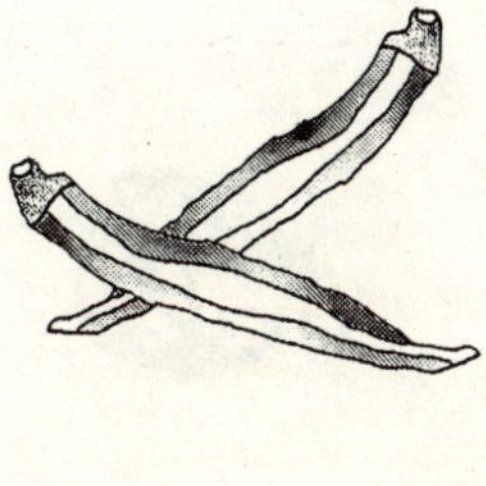

Maharashtra

Potato and Dill Salad

Serv 6

Ingredients

2 cups potatoes, boiled, cooled and cut into 1" cubes
1 tsp cumin seeds, roasted and coarsely crushed
1 tsp aniseed, roasted and slightly crushed
1 tsp salt
1 tsp coarsely ground black pepper
½ cup fresh dill (shepu), chopped
2 tsp lime juice

Method

Cut the potatoes into cubes while they are still warm. Add the cumin seeds, aniseed, salt and black pepper. Mix well and let stand for at least ½ hour. When the potatoes are cool, add the fresh dill and lime juice. Serve at room temperature.

Maharashtra

Fresh Fenugreek Salad

Serves 4

Ingredients

1 cup fresh fenugreek leaves, the smaller the better
½ tsp sugar
½ tsp salt
2 garlic cloves, crushed
1 green chilli, slit lengthwise
2 tbsp lime juice
½ cup fresh spinach, washed, pat dry with a cloth and chop
¼ cup green coriander, chopped
1 tsp peanut powder
1 tsp roasted sesame seeds

Method

Add salt, garlic, chilli and lemon juice to the sugar and stir until the sugar dissolves.

Wash and dry all the greens. Add the dressing, peanut powder and roasted sesame seeds to the greens. Serve immediately.

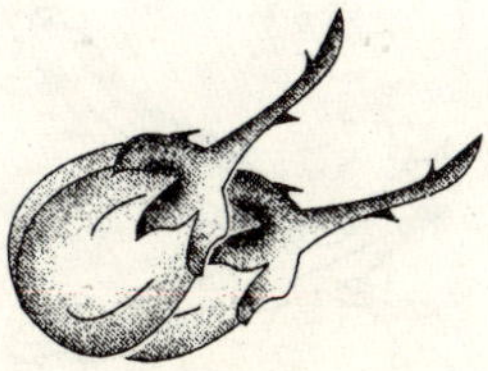

French Beans, Maharashtrian style

Serves 4

Ingredients

¼ kg French beans
2 tbsp lemon juice
1 tsp salt
½ tsp sugar
2 tbsp fresh grated coconut
1 tbsp chopped green coriander

Roast together on a tawa:
2 tsp white dal
1 tsp black mustard seeds
1 dry red chilli broken into pieces
6-8 curry leaves

Method

Wash and cut the beans into long strips (juliennes). Steam in a colander over boiling water until still crunchy (4-5 minutes). Remove and immerse in cold water or ice immediately to cool. This retains the colour and texture of the beans. Drain completely, add the lemon juice, salt, sugar and toss. Add rest of the ingredients and refrigerate. Serve chilled.

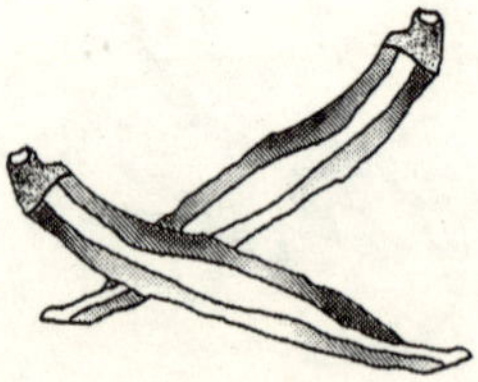

Beetroot and Orange Salad

Serves 6

Ingredients

500g fresh beetroot
2 large oranges
1 cup spring onions, cut into long, thin strips
½ cup pistachios roughly chopped (keep aside some for garnishing)
salt to taste
1 tsp coarsely ground black pepper
2 tsp black mustard seeds, roasted and coarsely ground
½ cup lime juice

Method

Wash and boil the beetroots whole with their skins, until tender (about 40 minutes in saucepan, 10 minutes in a pressure cooker). Check with a fork. Cool, peel and cut into 1" cubes. Peel the oranges and divide into segments, removing the skin. Add to the beetroot. Mix in all the other ingredients leaving some pistachios for the garnish. Serve at room temperature or chilled.

Quick Chickpea Salad

Serves 6

Ingredients

3 cups cooked chickpea
3 tsp tamarind pulp
1 green chilli chopped fine
1 tsp garlic paste
1 cup pomegranate seeds
1 cup spring onions, chopped fine
1 cup tomatoes, blanched, skinned and chopped roughly
½ tsp garam masala
½ cup fresh coriander
1 tbsp ginger, cut into fine strips
rock salt to taste

Method

Be warned that chickpea swells to about double its quantity after soaking. Make sure that you soak in plenty of water in a large bowl. 1 cup raw chickpea will give you approximately 3 cups after cooking.

Mix the tamarind, the green chilli and garlic with 3 or more tablespoons of warm water to form a dressing. Add to the chickpeas. Mix well. Stir in the pomegranate seeds, spring onions and tomatoes. Adjust seasoning. Serve garnished with garam masala, fresh coriander and ginger strips.

This is a nice quick salad or snack. Cooked chickpea will keep in the fridge (in a little water) for upto a week. You can replace the chickpea with cooked potatoes or any sprouted pulse like val (split white beans), kidney beans, black eyed beans or green chickpea. If using sprouted beans you need not soak overnight. Just steam until tender. For a non-vegetarian salad, substitute the chickpeas with the equivalent amount of roasted or steamed chicken, skin removed and cut into pieces.

Quick Potato Salads

Serves 4

Salad 1

Ingredients

2 tbsp tamarind pulp mixed with 2 tbsp water
1 tbsp jaggery
2 cups boiled potatoes, diced into 1" cubes
salt to taste
¼ tsp garam masala

Method

Mix the tamarind pulp and jaggery to a smooth paste. Add to the potatoes while they are still warm so that the flavours permeate the potatoes. Cool and add salt and garam masala.

Salad 2

Serves 4

Ingredients

2 cups boiled potatoes, diced into 1" cubes
1 tsp olive oil
½ cup green stalks from spring onions, chopped
salt and freshly ground pepper to taste
2 tbsp wholegrain mustard

Method

Mix the oil into the potatoes while they are still warm. This will prevent them from sticking later. Add the rest of the ingredients. Mix well and serve at room temperature.

My Nutty Rice Salad

Serves 6

Ingredients

4 cups cooked brown rice or basmati rice
½ cup celery, finely chopped
1 cup tomatoes, blanched, skinned and finely chopped
1 cup spring onions, with greens, finely chopped
1 cup together of roasted cashewnuts, roasted peanuts and roasted pumpkin or watermelon seeds

Dressing ingredients :
2 tsp salt
1 tsp freshly ground pepper
4 tbsp lemon juice
1 tsp sugar
½ cup orange juice
3 tsp wholegrain mustard
1 tbsp olive oil

Method

Put celery, tomatoes and spring onions in a bowl with the rice. For the dressing, mix all the ingredients in a bowl, pouring in the oil last. Stir until the sugar is dissolved. Add dressing to the vegetables and rice till well coated.
Garnish with nuts and pumpkin seeds which can vary according to your taste. Watermelon and melon seeds are also available at most dry fruit stores in India.
Serve at room temperature. Along with roasted tomato and cumin soup, this makes a complete meal.

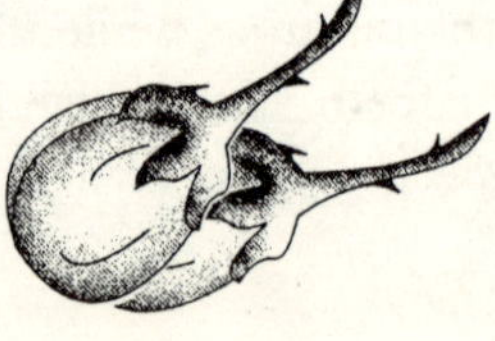

Karwar

Spinach and Yellow Dal Salad

Serves 6

Ingredients

½ kg cucumber, grated
½ cup grated coconut
½ cup yellow dal (soaked overnight) in water
1 small raw mango, peeled and grated
2 bunches or 300g spinach, roughly chopped
1 tsp finely chopped ginger
½ cup chopped (fresh) coriander
2-3 chopped green chillies
1 tsp mustard seeds (roasted on a tava)
1 tbsp cumin seeds (roasted on a tava)
8-10 curry leaves
1 tsp oil
salt to taste

Method

Remove the excess water from the grated cucumber by gentle squeezing. Add the grated coconut. Drain the water from the soaked yellow dal and wash in another change of water. Drain completely and add along with the raw grated mango, spinach, half the chopped ginger, half the chopped coriander and half the chopped chillies to the cucumber and coconut mixture. Fold all the ingredients together. Heat a tawa or hot griddle and add mustard, until it crackles. Add cumin seeds. Remove from heat. In a seasoning ladle, add 1 teaspoon oil. When hot, add the remaining ginger, green chilli and coriander. Finally, add the curry leaves. When well coated and cooked through remove and add to the cucumber mix with the mustard and cumin. Mix thoroughly and refrigerate. Add salt just before serving. If salt is added with the other seasoning it is likely to make the salad watery. Serve this salad chilled.

Carrot, Peanut and Raisin Salad

This is my all time favourite recipe for carrot salad. The carrots are slightly steamed to retain their colour and flavour and consequently the salad can be made well in advance. Left overs taste even better.

Serves 6

Ingredients

500g Mahabaleshwar (preferably) or any juicy carrots, peeled and cut into juliennes, (thin matchstick like strips). Do not grate to save time. You'll end up with a watery mess later.
½ cup raisins (kishmish)
½ cup roasted peanuts, roughly chopped
2 tbsp chopped coriander
2 tbsp sesame seeds, roasted

Dressing:

1 cup orange juice
½ cup lime juice
2 cloves garlic, crushed
1 tsp honey
1 tsp whole cumin seeds, roasted and coarsely crushed
salt and pepper to taste

Method

Mix all the dressing ingredients first. Steam the carrots. Cool. They should still be very crunchy and bright orange in colour. Refresh them with ice or put them in the fridge to cool. Soak the raisins in warm water for a few minutes. Drain the water. Mix all the salad ingredients with the dressing and raisins. It is not essential but preferable that the salad is chilled. If the carrots absorb all the dressing while being chilled, make some more dressing and add just before serving. A perfect accompaniment to spicy curries.

North India

Three Bean Chaat

Serves 6

Ingredients

½ cup kidney beans
½ cup black eyed beans
½ cup chickpeas
1 tsp chaat masala
2 tbsp lime juice
1 cup fresh coriander
2 white onions finely chopped or 1 cup spring onions
2 tomatoes finely chopped
½ cup fresh pomegranate seeds
salt to taste

Method

Soak the beans separately overnight. Drain, wash in several changes of water and boil each of the beans separately with salt. You will get approximately double the quantity of the beans when cooked. Cool and drain. Place all the drained beans in a bowl. Add the remaining ingredients and toss. Serve at room temperature with date and tamarind chutney and cucumber and mint raita.

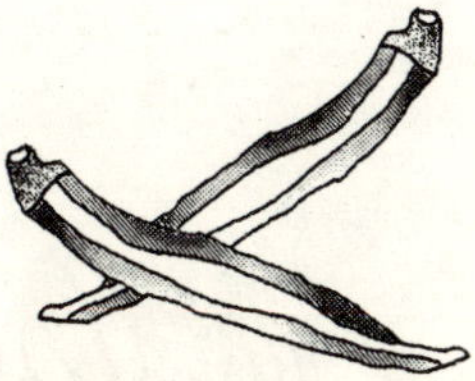

Dry Prawn Relish

Serves 4

Ingredients

1 cup dried prawns (small variety)
3 red Kashmiri chillies, coarsely crushed
1 medium sized onion, finely chopped
¼ cup grated coconut
salt to taste
2 tbsp lime juice

Method

Clean the prawns (top and tail). Roast them on a tawa until crisp. Mix in red chillies, onion and coconut. Add salt and lime juice to taste. Serve as a relish with prawn or fish curry and rice.

Malabar Prawns

Serves 4

Ingredients

½ kg raw jumbo prawns, peeled and deveined
leave the tail intact
2 tbsp lime juice
1 tsp salt
1 tbsp garlic paste
2 tbsp Malabar masala (pg. 32)
1 cup rice flour
1 tbsp olive oil
2 tbsp grated coconut, lightly roasted

Method

Mix the prawns with lime juice, salt and garlic paste. Leave to marinate for 10 minutes. Remove the excess liquid. Coat with the Malabar masala and then roll lightly in the rice flour. Grill under a preheated grill turning the prawns once. Brush with a little olive oil. Serve piping hot, garnished with the roasted grated coconut.

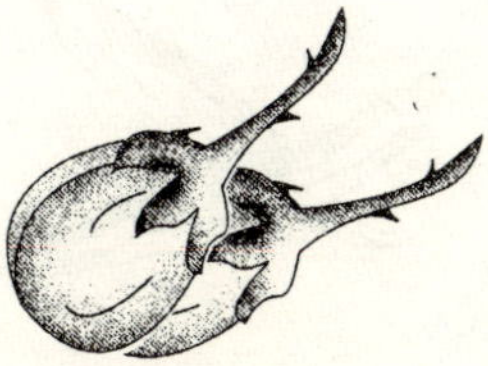

Prawns in Coconut Lime Sauce

Serves 6

Ingredients

½ kg large white prawns, peeled and deveined
2 tsp salt
2 tsp sugar
5 tbsp lime juice
½ cup thick coconut milk (consistency of cream)
3 spring onions, thinly sliced
2 green chillies chopped
1 tbsp chopped fresh coriander

Method

Toss the prawns with 1 teaspoon salt. Leave for 10 minutes. Rinse in cold water. Drain and pat dry. Toss with the sugar, lime juice and remaining salt in a bowl and leave to marinate for 10 minutes. Arrange the prawns and their marinade in a heatproof dish, pour the coconut cream over them and microwave on high for 4 minutes or in a medium hot oven for 10 minutes until the prawns turn pink.

Garnish with spring onions, chillies and coriander. This can be eaten cold either as a salad or starter or served warm as a main dish with a little rice.

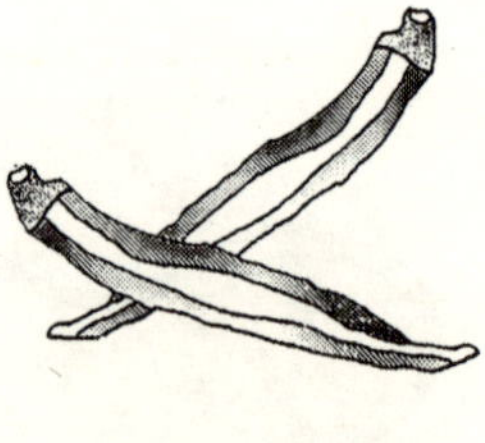

North India

Traditional Chicken Tikka

Serves 4

Ingredients

600g boneless chicken

1½ cups hung curd (yogurt hung in a muslin cloth until the water drains out, 2-4 hours)

½ tsp chilli powder

1 tsp garam masala

2 tsp crushed ginger

1½ tsp crushed garlic

2 tsp lemon juice

1 tsp salt

a pinch of dry mango powder

1 tbsp oil

Method

Cut the chicken into 1½" cubes. Combine the hung curd, chilli powder, garam masala, ginger, garlic, lemon juice and salt and mix into the chicken. Leave to marinate for 2-3 hours. Thread the chicken on skewers. Cook over charcoal or under a very hot grill for 10-12 minutes, turning once, basting with oil until cooked and golden brown. Sprinkle with dry mango powder. Serve with mint chutney, onion rings and lemon wedges.

Helpful hint — Drain all the water from the chicken pieces and wipe dry before adding the marinade. This is to prevent the marinade from becoming diluted and losing its flavour.

Malabar Style Clams

Serves 4

Ingredients

1 kg clams with shell
2 medium sized onions, whole
8 cloves roasted garlic
½ cup chicken stock
½ cup fresh grated coconut
1 tbsp Malabar masala (pg. 32)
salt to taste

Method

Roast the onions and a whole garlic pod in a moderate oven for 30 minutes. Remove the outer skin and slice the onion. Remove around 8 cloves of garlic, peel and crush. Wash the clams in several changes of water. In a large wok, throw in the onions, garlic, stock and coconut. Stir for a few minutes. Add the Malabar masala and clams, drained of their water. Stir well. Cover the pan with a lid and steam until the clams have opened. Mix well. Clams tend to be salty so tasting is essential at this stage. Do not eat the clams which have remained closed after steaming.

Serve with hot crusty bread to dunk into the sauce.

Maharashtra

Tomato Saar (Tomato and Coconut Soup)

Serves 4

Ingredients

700g tomatoes
1 tbsp rice flour or plain white flour (maida)
1½ cups coconut milk
8-10 curry leaves
1 fresh green chilli, finely chopped
½ tsp salt
a pinch of sugar
a pinch of freshly ground black pepper
1 tbsp finely chopped fresh, green coriander

Method

Drop the tomatoes into boiling water for 15 seconds. Remove and peel. Chop up the tomatoes and put them into a small pan. Cover and simmer for about 15 minutes or until the tomatoes are soft. Put the tomatoes into a blender and mix until smooth. Put the rice flour or maida into a bowl. Slowly add the coconut milk, mixing as you go, to avoid lumps. Put this liquid into the food processor or a blender and blend with the tomatoes. Pour the mixture into a saucepan or handi and bring to a simmer. Throw in the curry leaves and the chopped green chilli. Stir once. Add salt, sugar and black pepper. Cook, uncovered, for about 5 minutes stirring every now and then. Traditionally this dish is served hot but it is equally delicious served chilled with an ice cube. Garnish with fresh chopped coriander. If the tomatoes are very pulpy, you may need to add a little water when blending.

Chilled Mango and Orange Soup

Serves 4

Ingredients

2 tbsp cornflour
½ cup water
2 glasses fresh orange juice or unsweetned orange juice
4 fresh mangoes (peeled de-seeded and mashed) or 400g frozen mango pulp, unsweetened
a pinch of cinnamon powder
1 tsp Madras curry powder
salt to taste
2 tbsp coriander leaves
2 tbsp thick whipped yogurt

Method

Combine the cornflour with a few tablespoons of water and blend to a smooth paste. Stir in the orange juice slowly and place over a low gas flame. When the liquid starts to thicken and boil, take it off the flame and stir in the mango, cinammon powder, Madras curry powder and salt. Chill in the fridge for at least 1 hour. Serve chilled garnished with fresh coriander leaves (not chopped) and yogurt, drizzled on top.

If you use orange juice from a tin or carton (which in India is usually sweetened), choose a variety of mango which is less sweet.

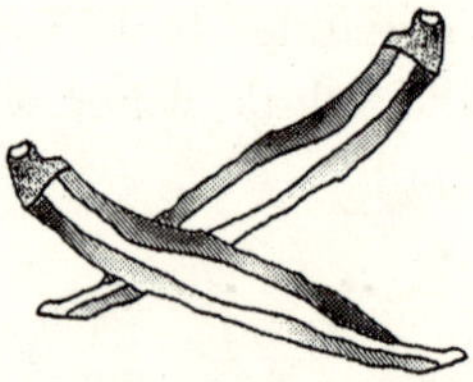

South India

Rasam (soup)

Serves 6

Ingredients

½ kg large ripe tomatoes, peeled chopped
1 tbsp tamarind pulp
¼ cup yellow split dal
1 large onion, sliced
3 cloves of garlic, crushed
8 coriander stalks
3 tsp Sambhar Masala (pg. 31)
7½ cups water
¼ cup coriander leaves (do not chop)
10 curry leaves
¼ tsp roasted black mustard seeds
¼ tsp roasted fenugreek seeds
2-3 tbsp cooked rice (optional)

Method

Put all the ingredients except the dal, coriander leaves, curry leaves, roasted mustard and fenugreek into a large pan. Bring to the boil and then simmer for 20 minutes to half an hour and strain through a fine sieve. Boil the dal with 1 cup water until the dal is very soft. Add the rasam water to the dal and simmer for a further 5 minutes. Season with salt if needed. Serve piping hot, garnished with the coriander leaves, curry leaves, the roasted mustard and fenugreek.

For a more substantial soup which can be a one course, quick lunch, use ½ cup of yellow split dal and add to the rasam water as above. In this case, you really don't need to strain the spices out at all. Add a few tablespoons of cooked rice to the soup.

Tomato and Roasted Cumin Soup

Serves 6

Ingredients

2 kg ripe tomatoes
a pinch of sugar
2 medium onions
8 garlic cloves
1 large, fresh red chilli (hot) or 1 tsp red chilli powder
2 tbsp whole cumin seeds, roasted and ground (fine)
2 cups tomato juice
salt to taste
a pinch of freshly ground black pepper
1 tsp whole, roasted cumin seeds for garnish

Method

Slice the tomatoes in half and sprinkle with a little sugar. Put them on a sheet of foil in a hot oven for about 1 hour or until they are dehydrated and have caramelised slightly. Remove the tomatoes from the baking sheet and set aside. Roughly chop the onions, garlic, and chilli. Add the ground cumin, tomatoes and the tomato juice and cook on a slow fire for 15 to 20 minutes. You may need to add a little water. Puree in a blender until smooth. Adjust seasoning (salt and freshly ground pepper). Serve hot garnished with whole roasted cumin.

Chilled Melon and Prawn Soup

Serves 4

Ingredients

2 medium sized cantaloupe or honeydew melons
½ cup chicken stock (warm)
1 cup whipped yogurt
1 tbsp lime juice
salt to taste
12 large prawns, peeled and cooked (poach or steam) with their tails

Method

Cut the melons in half crosswise and discard the pips. Scoop out most of the pulp carefully. Place the flesh in a mixer with the stock. Puree until smooth. Blend in the yogurt and the lime juice. Season to taste with salt. Pour the puree into the melon shells and add the prawns. Chill before serving.

South India

Kerala Clam & Shrimp Soup

Serves 4

Ingredients

600g clams in their shell
150g shrimps, after removing shell and deveining
3 onions, finely chopped
10 curry leaves
6 cloves garlic (crushed with flat of a knife and finely chopped)
1" piece of ginger, finely chopped
2 stalks celery, finely chopped
1½ tsp red chilli paste (dry red Kashmiri chilli made into a paste with water in a mixer,
2½ cups prawn or chicken stock
salt to taste
4 tsp lime juice
½ cup coconut milk
1 cup water

The masala

1 tsp black peppercorns
½ tsp black mustard seeds
2 tsp coriander seeds
A small pinch fenugreek seeds

Method

Roast the pepper, mustard, coriander and fenugreek seeds, individually, over low heat. Remove to a mortar or grinding stone, and grind into a fine powder (if using a grinder, grind with very short pulses, opening the lid each time). In a heavy bottomed saucepan, add onions, curry leaves, garlic, ginger, celery and a few tablespoons of water and cook until translucent and glossy. Add the dry roasted masala and red chilli paste. Cook, adding small quantities of water if necessary, to prevent sticking. The colour of the mixture will darken as you cook it. Now add the prawn stock, bring to a boil, reduce to low heat and simmer, stirring at regular intervals, until reduced by a quarter. Add clams, shrimps and salt, simmer for 2 minutes. Add lime juice, stir, add coconut milk and bring to just under a boil, ensuring that it does not come to a bubble (or the coconut milk will curdle). Remove and adjust the seasoning.

Serve hot with crisp garlic naan or garlic bread.

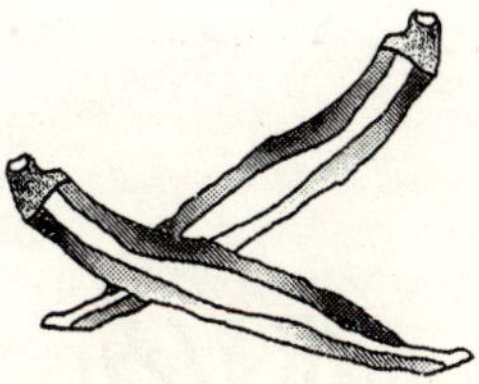

North India

Smoked Aubergine Pate
(Lean Baingan ka Bharta)

Serves 6

Ingredients

1½ kg large aubergines
1 tsp cumin seeds, roasted
1 large onion, finely chopped
1 tbsp finely grated ginger
1 tbsp finely chopped garlic
4 tomatoes, skinned and chopped
3 green chillies, finely chopped
2 tbsp whipped yogurt
salt to taste
1 cup fresh coriander finely chopped

Method

Make a few slits in the aubergines and roast each over a medium gas flame until the skin has charred all over. Alternatively score and put them in a hot oven for about 25 minutes, or until the aubergines are soft. The first method is more laborious but the flavour is better. Cool. Discard the skin and mash the flesh with the back of a fork. Add all the other ingredients to the mashed aubergine. Mix well. Serve at room temperature along with hot tandoori roti and a raita.

Fresh Mint Chutney

A great addition to any Indian table. Can also be used as a salad dressing and sandwich spread. The only problem is that you cannot store it for too long, even in the fridge, since it will darken on top. The following will make 1 cup of chutney.

Ingredients

2 cups fresh mint leaves (no stalks)
2 cups fresh coriander (no stalks)
4 green chillies
4 tbsp lime juice
1 tsp of sugar
1 tsp salt
1" piece ginger, peeled and chopped

Method

Put all ingredients in a blender / grinder and puree until smooth. You may need to add a little water. Adjust the seasoning and refrigerate until needed. For a thicker chutney, add 2 tablespoons grated, fresh coconut while blending.

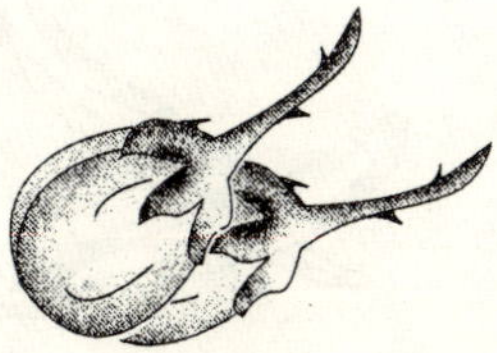

Date and Tamarind Chutney
(makes 2 cups of chutney)

Ingredients

½ tsp red chilli powder
4 tbsp thick tamarind pulp
½ cup jaggery
4 cups water
1 tsp finely chopped ginger
¼ tsp cumin
½ cup dates, de-seeded. Cut into 4, lengthwise
½ tsp cloves
2" cinnamon stick
1 tsp rock salt

Method

Put all ingredients together in a pan on a medium flame and bring to a boil. Simmer for about 10 minutes or until the ingredients are soft and pulpy. Sieve through a fine strainer. Put back on fire and cook on a low flame until it becomes the consistency of a thick custard. It should be reduced by half i.e. 2 cups chutney. This will take approximately 15 minutes. Adjust seasoning. Cool and serve with any chaat, salad or raita. The chutney will keep in the fridge for weeks.

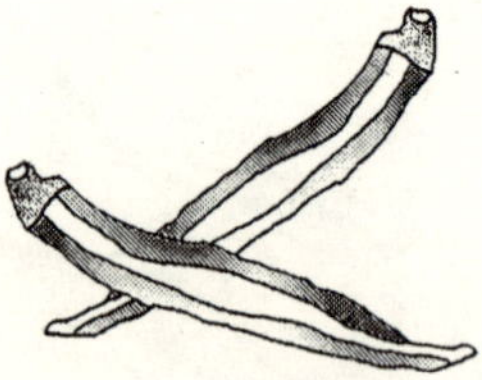

Tomato Chutney

Ingredients

1 kg tomatoes
1 onion (preferably a mild, white one)
5 cloves garlic (whole, small)
1 tsp ginger (grated)
½ tsp wild onion seeds
¼ tsp coriander seeds
½" piece cinnamon
4 cloves
1 tsp chilli powder
2 black cardamoms
½ cup of either or all of following : kishmish, dates, dried apricots
½ cup vinegar (preferably sugarcane or good malt vinegar)
1 cup jaggery

Method

Plunge the tomatoes into boiling water for a few seconds. Remove the skin and chop roughly reserving all the pulp and juice. Firm, red tomatoes are best for this chutney. Put all the tomatoes into a large casserole. Add all the spices, vinegar and jaggery and bring to a boil. Simmer until the chutney thickens. (This will depend upon the tomatoes. It could take anywhere between 10-15 minutes) Add the dry fruit (kishmish, dates, dried apricots). Cook for a further 5-10 minutes. Take care that the chutney does not stick to the bottom of the pan, by stirring continuously. Fill while the mixture is still very hot into sterilised glass jars and shut the lid tight. This method should form a vacuum which will increase the shelf life of the chutney. Alternatively, allow the chutney to cool completely and bottle. If you use the second method you may need to refrigerate the chutney at all times. The above method would make about 2 bottles of chutney.

Oil Free Lemon Pickle

Besides being a great pickle, lemon pickle makes a delicious spicy dressing when added to raw vegetables like bitter gourd or grated cucumber.

Ingredients

25 limes
¼ kg green chillies
½ cup salt
1 tsp turmeric
1 tbsp split, yellow mustard seeds
1 tbsp fenugreek seeds
3 tbsp red chilli powder
1 kg sugar or jaggery
1 tsp whole black peppercorn

Method

Cut the lime and chillies into bite sized chunks. Put into a flat container or thali, sprinkle with salt and turmeric and leave in the sun or in a warm place for 2-3 hours or until the salt melts. Transfer to a heavy bottomed utensil and cook gently until the mixture begins to boil. Then simmer until the lime skins are tender (could take upto 2 hours). Stir in the spices and sugar or jaggery and cook for a further 10 minutes. Cool and bottle or pour in hot into sterilised glass jars.

Traditionally, the limes are left for 15 to 20 days in the sun or in a warm place with the salt and turmeric. They are shaken every day. The spices are added, stirred well and left again for a further 5 days. The pickle is therefore never cooked and is totally oil free. It keeps for years. For those of us who do not have the time, patience or sunlight to do all this, you now have an alternative method.

Cucumber and Mint Raita

Serves 6

Ingredients

2 cups yogurt, lightly whisked
½ tsp sugar
1 tsp garlic paste
1 cup hung curd
1 cup fresh mint, chopped (leave aside a few sprigs for garnish)
2 cups grated cucumber
1 cup spring onions, chopped
salt to taste
salt and freshly ground black pepper to taste
a few sprigs of mint leaves
½ tsp cumin seeds, roasted and powdered

Method

Whisk together the yogurt, sugar, garlic and hung curd until smooth. Add the mint, cucumber (gently squeezed of its water) and spring onions. Mix well. Add salt and pepper. Chill and serve garnished with a few springs of mint and roasted cumin powder.

The hung curd gives the raita a body. Cucumber tends to retain water even after squeezing. This method with the addition of hung curd, ensures that the raita will remain thick and not turn up something resembling lassi.

Karwar

Lady Finger and Mustard Raita

Serves 6

Ingredients

½ kg ladyfinger (okra)
½ cup fresh coconut, grated
2 tbsp mustard seeds, roasted
½ cup fresh coriander, chopped
4-6 green chillies, chopped
1 tsp oil
½ kg yogurt, whisked until smooth
salt to taste
a pinch of asafoetida
1 tbsp cumin seeds, roasted
8-10 curry leaves, roasted

Method

Blend the grated coconut, 1 tablespoon of the mustard seeds, chopped coriander and chopped green chillies to a fine paste with a little water. Cut the lady fingers into very small pieces and stir fry in 1 teaspoon oil till semi-crisp. Allow to cool. Add yogurt to the coconut masala and puree in a blender. Season with salt. Add the chopped lady fingers to the masala mixture in a bowl by hand. Roast the remaining mustard, asafoetida, cumin seeds and curry leaves on a hot tawa or griddle until the aroma changes and mustard seeds begin to crackle. Pour onto the ladyfinger mixture. Mix well. Serve chilled.

This can be served as a salad, dip or as an accompaniment to south Indian dishes.

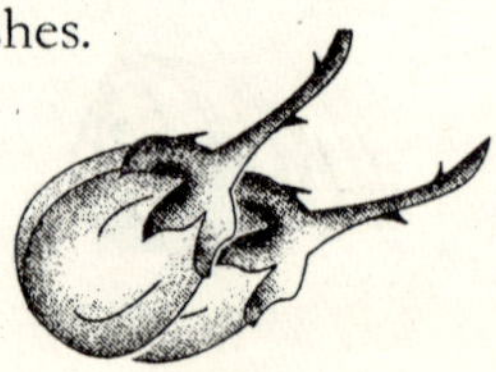

Red Pumpkin Raita

Serves 4

Ingredients

¼ kg red pumpkin (lal bhopla), peeled and cut into 1" cubes
1 cup yogurt, whisked until smooth
1 tbsp fresh grated coconut or 1 tsp desiccated coconut
½ tsp salt
½ tsp sugar
2 green chillies, slit lengthwise
1 tbsp peanut powder
2 tbsp fresh coriander, chopped
½ tsp cumin, roasted and coarsely crushed

Method

Steam the pumpkin in a colander over boiling water until just done (approximately 7-9 minutes). Cool. Add the yogurt, grated coconut, salt, sugar and green chillies. Mix thoroughly. Garnish with peanut powder, fresh coriander and roasted cumin.
Serve at room temperature.

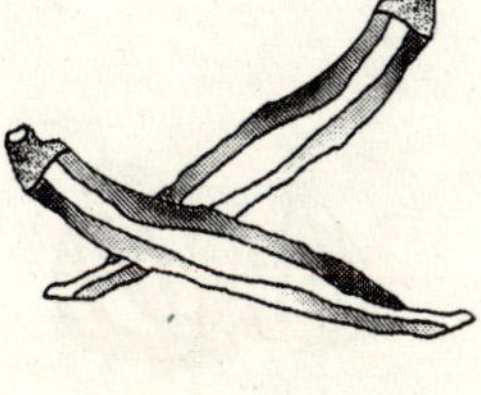

Pineapple Raita

Serves 4

Ingredients

2 cups fresh pineapple cut into 1" cubes
2 tbsp grated fresh coconut
½ tsp ground cumin
1 cup thick yogurt, whisked until smooth
½ tsp salt

Roast
½ tsp red / brown mustard seeds
2 dry red chillies, broken into pieces
8-10 curry leaves

Method

Grind to a paste with a little water, the coconut and cumin. Add to the pineapple and stir this into the yogurt. Add all the other ingredients. The tempering ingredients are traditionally cooked in 1 tablespoon coconut oil and then poured onto the raita just before serving. You can roast them instead and throw it over the raita if you would like to avoid the oil altogether. Serve chilled.

Maharashtra

Guava Raita

Serves 4

Ingredients

2 cups green guavas, de-seeded and diced into ½" cubes
1 cup thick yogurt hung in a muslin cloth if necessary
1 tsp green chilli paste (chilli blended with water to a fine paste)
salt to taste

Method

Make sure you choose guavas which are not too ripe otherwise the whole dish will turn into something resembling baby food. Mix the diced guavas into the yogurt along with the green chilli paste and salt. Serve at room temperature or chilled.

Guavas make a delightful salad or chaat. They take very well to salty and spicy seasoning and make a perfect accompaniment to Indian vegetarian dishes.

Maharashtra

Carrot Koshimbir

Serves 3

Ingredients

2 cups coarsely grated carrot
1 tbsp coarsely ground roasted peanuts
1 tbsp jaggery
1 tbsp tamarind pulp
1 tsp green chilli, made into a paste
salt to taste

Roast
a pinch of asafoetida
1 tsp mustard seeds

Method

The traditional oil tadka or tempering of asafoetida and mustard can be replaced by roasting the spices. Mix all the ingredients leaving aside the roasted spices. Make sure that the jaggery is mixed to a smooth paste with the tamarind pulp and a little warm water. This will form the dressing since there is no oil. Add the roasted spices and the dressing to the carrot mixture. Mix well and serve at room temperature. Carrot koshimbir is a perfect accompaniment to Maharashtrian vegetarian dishes.

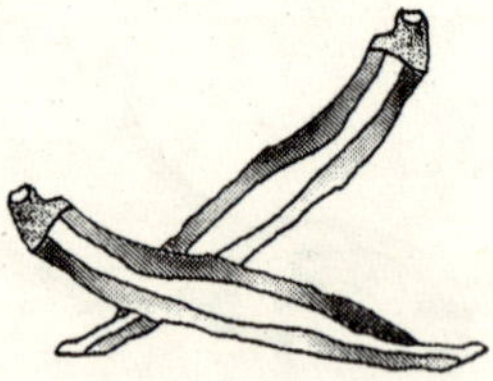

Maharashtra

Cucumber Koshimbir

Serves 3

Ingredients

2 cups coarsely grated cucumber
1 tsp lime juice
1 tsp salt
1 tsp sugar
1 tbsp coarsely crushed roasted peanuts
1 tsp grated fresh coconut
2 green chillies, chopped fine
1 tbsp fresh coriander, chopped fine

Method

Squeeze out all the water from the grated cucumber. Mix the lime juice, salt and sugar together in a bowl. Add all the remaining ingredients. Serve at room temperature. Cucumber koshimbir in a perfect accompaniment to Maharashtrian vegetarian dishes.

Konkan

Kokum Saar

Serves 2

Ingredients

4 cups water
6-8 pieces kokum (more if the kokum is dry)
salt to taste
¼ tsp grated ginger
1 onion chopped fine
2 green chillies, slit
1 tbsp fresh coriander, chopped fine

Method

Boil the kokum for 10 minutes. Cool. Strain the liquid. Add salt, ginger, onion, chillies and coriander and refrigerate until needed. Kokum saar can be kept for at least a couple of weeks in the fridge. It is an excellent appetiser, popular on the Konkan coast to cool down the effect of those fiery fish curries.

I also serve it with steamed seafood and with raw oysters instead of lemon or any vinegar based dressing.

Sol kadi is a derivative, which can be served in the same way. Here kokum pieces are added to coconut milk (no heat) along with salt, a hint of garlic and green chillis. The mixture is left to infuse for at least 5-10 minutes. It is strained and can be served garnished with chopped coriander and is best served very chilled.

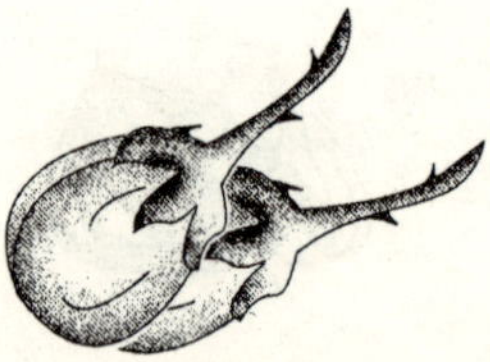

Roasted Brinjal Relish

Serves 4

Ingredients

2 large dark purple brinjals

½ cup coconut cream made by blending the white of tender green coconut with its water in a blender

Salt to taste

1 tbsp chopped fresh coriander

½ cup puffed rice (poha) soaked in water for five minutes and drained

Roast

2 dry red chillies broken into pieces

1 tsp mustard seeds

a pinch of asafoetida

Method

Roast the brinjal in the oven or over a gas flame until the skin is charred and the flesh is soft. When cool enough to handle, remove the skin. Mash the flesh with a fork and add all the ingredients and roasted spices. The coconut cream can be replaced with canned or thick fresh coconut milk, but it does have a delicate, distinct taste of its own.

Serve at room temperature as a dip or as a salad.

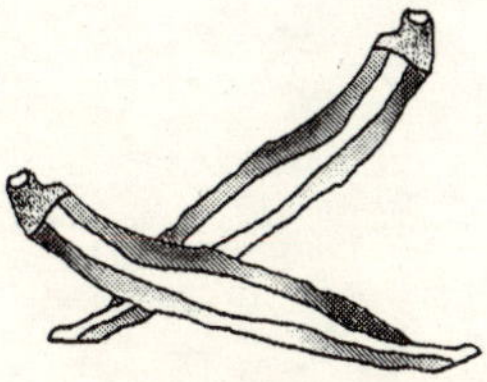

Vegetarian

Main Course

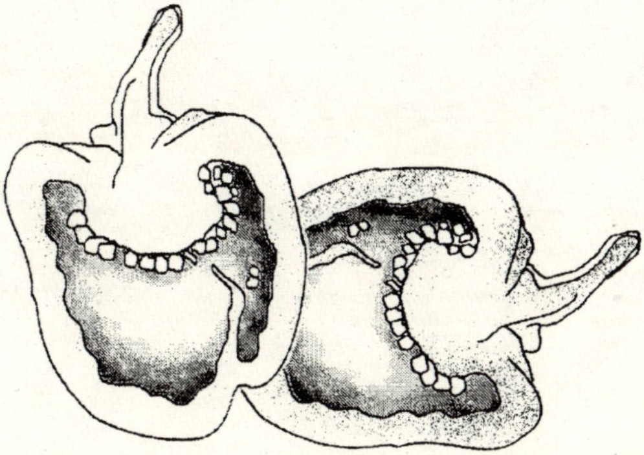

Karwar

Madras Cucumber/Pumpkin Curry

Serves 6-8

Ingredients

1 kg magai kai (Madras cucumber)
2 tbsp cumin
a pinch of asafoetida
3 red chilli (Bedge) whole
8 cups water
salt to taste
2 tbsp jaggery
3 green chillies
1 thick lemon grass stalk chopped into 4 and bruised or ½ cup chopped tomatoes
4 cups coconut milk
¼ cup yogurt whisked until smooth
1 ½ tsp mustard seeds roasted
8-10 curry leaves roasted
2-3 red chillies roasted and broken into pieces

Method

Prepare the masala by grinding the whole cumin, asafoetida and red chilli in a mixer to a fine paste. Peel magai kai, de-seed and cut into 1½" cubes. Boil magai kai cubes in 8 cups of water, 1 teaspoon salt, jaggery and green chillies. When the pumpkin cubes are a little more than half cooked, remove them from the water. The liquid should have reduced to less than half. Strain the liquid and add the masala paste to the water in which you have boiled the pumpkin. Bring this to a boil. Add the coconut milk and lemon grass. Lower the flame and add the whisked yogurt. Stir for a minute or so and add the pumpkin. Roast the mustard seeds, the curry leaves and red chillies. Remove the mustard seeds when they begin to crackle. When the red chillies starts changing colour, remove from the heat and add all three to the pumpkin curry. Serve hot with steamed rice.

Tomatoes are added towards the end of cooking in the original recipe to add a little sour taste and colour. I like to add chopped lemon grass stalks for that added fragrance. In the original recipe, grated coconut is blended with the spices and ground to a fine paste before water is added for a coconut cream consistency. Nowadays, grating and blending fresh coconut can be laborious. I prefer to use readymade coconut cream or milk. It makes the job easier, quicker and you get a perfect, velvet smooth curry every time.

Karwar

Auray Kai Palya
(Steamed Long Green Beans)

Serves 6-8

Ingredients

1 kg long green beans (auray kai) or French beans
18-20 garlic cloves
½ tbsp mustard seeds
1 tbsp oil
½ tsp turmeric
15 curry leaves
5 red chillies (Bedge, broken into pieces)
salt to taste
2 tbsp tamarind paste
1 tsp chilli powder

Method

Cut beans in ½" dices. Prepare the masala by grinding the garlic with mustard seeds. Remember to add the garlic last so that the mustard seeds do not stick whole to the moist paste. Heat the oil in seasoning ladle. Add turmeric, curry leaves and red chillies. Stir well until the red chillies change colour. Mix the masala with the seasoning in a kadhai or wok and stir on low fire until the smell of garlic fills the air. Add beans, salt, tamarind paste and chilli powder. Add a little water, cover and cook on a slow fire till the beans are cooked but slightly crunchy.

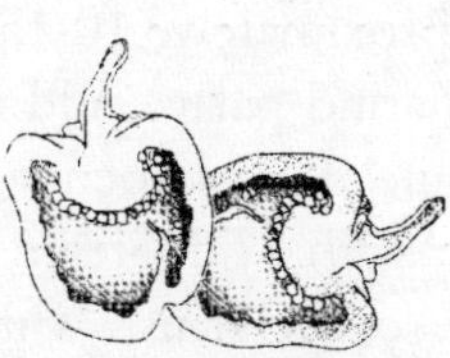

Karwar

Badnay Kai Palya
(Steam Cooked Brinjal Curry)

Serves 6

Ingredients

1 kg brinjal, medium size, purple/white
2 tbsp coriander seeds
½ tsp fenugreek seeds
4 dry red chillies, broken into pieces
salt to taste
1 tsp mustard seeds
1 tbsp white dal
a pinch of asafoetida
¼ tsp turmeric
10 curry leaves
2 cups sliced onions
3 cups tomatoes, chopped
1 ½ tbsp tamarind paste
½ cup fresh coriander, chopped

Method

Prepare the masala by roasting coriander, fenugreek and red chillies individually. Cool and crush to a coarse texture. Cut the brinjal into 1" cubes. Sprinkle with salt and leave for ½ hour. Squeeze out the water. This removes any bitterness or astringency from the brinjal. Roast the mustard and white dal, asafoetida, turmeric and curry leaves on a tawa. Put the onions and tomatoes together in a large wok. Add the first roasted spices and cook on a low flame until the mixture is soft and pulpy (approximately. 10-15 minutes). Add the brinjals, salt and tamarind paste. Add a little water and the roasted mustard, white dal, asafoetida, turmeric and curry leaves. Stir and cover with a lid. Steam cook on a low flame until the brinjals are soft. Garnish with chopped coriander.

Goa

Raw Mango Curry

Serves 6

Ingredients

4 medium sized tender green kairi mangoes, kairi (peeled and sliced with the seed)
4 cups water
¾ cup jaggery
1 tsp cumin seeds
½ tsp turmeric, ground
2 cloves
2 cardamoms
1" piece of cinnamon
1 tsp red chilli powder
salt to taste

Method

Grind the cumin, turmeric, cloves, cardamom and cinnamon to a fine powder on a grinding stone.

Heat 4 cups of water in a handi or large saucepan. Add the jaggery. Stir until it has dissolved. Add the raw mango and all the spices and simmer for approximately 20-30 minutes. Salt to taste. This is a poor man's curry eaten with boiled (steamed) rice and fried fish and is designed to combat the summer heat.

Karwar

Kai Rasa Pineapple Curry

Serves 6

Ingredients

1½ cup raw peanuts soaked and boiled
2 tbsp chickpea dal
2½ tbsp white dal
2½ tbsp yellow dal
1½ tbsp coriander seeds whole
1 tsp fenugreek seeds
3 red chillies broken into pieces
2 tbsp sesame seeds
1½ cups grated coconut
1 large pineapple, cleaned and diced into 1" pieces (not too ripe)
2 tbsp tamarind paste
6 cups of water
3-4 tbsp jaggery
1½ tsp mustard seeds
2 pinches asafoetida
½ tsp turmeric
8-10 curry leaves
salt to taste

Method

Soak the peanuts overnight, boil and cool (Alternatively use dry roasted peanuts). Prepare the masala by roasting the dals, coriander seeds, fenugreek seeds, red chillies and sesame seeds individually. Blend all these roasted spices and the coconut in a mixer until smooth. Boil the pineapple with the tamarind paste and 6 cups of water until soft but firm. Add boiled peanuts, jaggery and salt. Add the masala to the boiled pineapple. Bring to a boil and simmer. Meanwhile, roast each seasoning beginning with the mustard seeds, asafoetida, turmeric and curry leaves till they smoke. Pour onto the pineapple curry. Serve hot with steamed rice.

Grated coconut can be replaced with coconut milk. In that case, reduce the amount of water in which the pineapple is to be boiled to 4 cups. Grind the roasted spices together and add the coconut milk after the masala is added to the pineapple and boiled as with Madras cucumber curry.

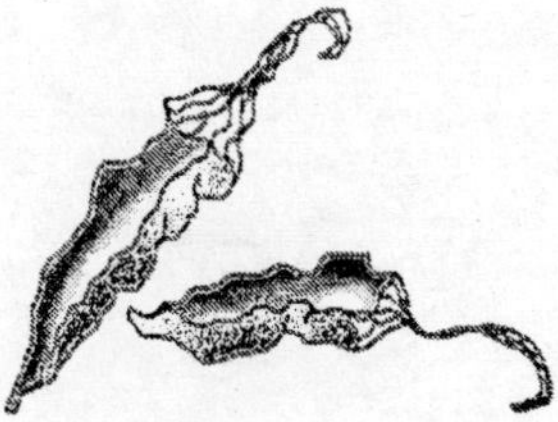

Potatoes, South Indian Style

Serves 6

Ingredients

1 kg potatoes (traditionally whole baby potatoes) boiled with their skins, peeled and chopped into 1" pieces
2 tsp Sambhar masala (pg. 31)
2 tsp roasted together fenugreek seeds, black mustard seeds, a pinch of asafoetida
10 curry leaves
½ cup water
½ cup fresh coriander or parsley, chopped
6 cloves garlic, crushed coarsely
1 tsp olive oil

Method

Put all the ingredients, except the parsley and garlic in a wok with half a cup of water on a slow flame. Stir continuously for 5 to 10 minutes or until all the potatoes are well coated with the spices. Add the coriander or parsley and continue cooking for two minutes. The parsley should still be green and slightly crunchy. Heat the oil and add the garlic. Cook until it turns golden and sprinkle on the potatoes. Serve hot with chapatis and a cool raita or plain yogurt. This dish is also delicious served at room temperature as a starter or snack.

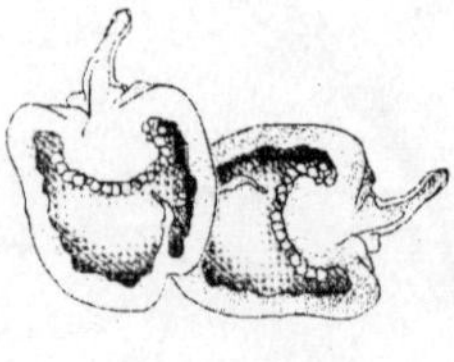

Cauliflower, South Indian Style

Serves 6

Ingredients

1 kg cauliflower broken into florets, washed and steamed until still crunchy
3 large tomatoes, blanched, peeled and chopped
2 large onions, diced
2" piece of ginger cut into long strips
8 cloves of garlic, crushed
2 tsp Sambhar masala (pg. 31)
1 tsp of roasted fenugreek and mustard seeds
8-10 curry leaves
2 tbsp chopped coriander
2 tsp grated fresh coconut

Method

Put the tomatoes, onions, ginger, garlic and sambhar masala in a wok and simmer for 5 minutes stirring occasionally. Add the cauliflower, roasted spices, curry leaves and stir well. Add 1 cup of water. Cover the pan and simmer until the cauliflower is cooked. The sauce and spices should stick to the cauliflower but not be completely dry. Garnish with coriander leaves and freshly grated coconut.

Maharashtra

Kolhapuri Style Brinjal

Serves 4

Ingredients

½ kg small brinjals, slit crosswise

Grind to a fine paste the following:
2 large onions
½ cup dry coconut, grated, lightly roasted till golden
1 tsp garlic paste
1 tsp ginger paste
½ cup fresh, chopped coriander
2 tsp Kolhapuri masala (pg. 31)

For the curry
½ tsp ginger-garlic paste
1 onion, chopped fine
1 cup water
salt to taste

Method

Grind onions, coconut, garlic paste, ginger paste, coriander and Kolhapuri masala to a fine paste. Fill this in the cross slits of the brinjals. Place them in a large skillet or wok with a cup of water, ginger-garlic paste, a chopped onion and salt to taste. Cook covered on a medium flame until tender (about 10 minutes).

Variation

This recipe is also excellent with prawns, either dry or fresh. If you are using dry prawns, grind them along with the masala paste which you stuff into the brinjals. If you are using fresh prawns, add them at the end of cooking stirred into the gravy. For dry prawns, you will need 3 tablespoons (small variety). For fresh prawns, choose small ones, about 200g which you peel and devein completely.

Kolhapuri Style Vegetables

You can also replace the brinjal in Kolhapuri style brinjal with mixed vegetables — cauliflower, peas and potatoes. The other ingredients remain the same. Use steamed vegetables and add a pinch of asafoetida to the dish towards the end of cooking.

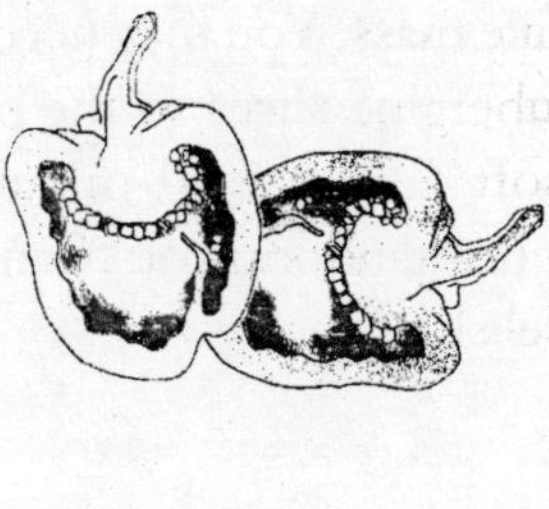

Pickled Aubergine with Cashews

Serves 4

Ingredients

2 large aubergines (approximately ½ kg), dark purple
2 tsp salt
½ tsp turmeric
1 tsp oil
1" ginger, grated
4 cloves garlic, finely chopped
2 onions, thinly sliced
2½ tsps cumin seeds, roasted and ground
1 tbsp fennel seeds, roasted and ground
2 tbsp black mustard seeds, roasted and ground roughly
1 tbsp chilli powder
1 cup malt vinegar
1 tbsp sugar
¼ cup raisins (kishmish)
¼ cup toasted cashews, whole
2 cups water

Method

Cut the aubergine into ¾" thick round slices and brush with salt and turmeric. Leave for 10 minutes. Drain water if any (don't squeeze). Place in a hot oven for 10 minutes. Brush very lightly with the oil. Meanwhile, mix all the remaining ingredients in a pan with 2 cups of water and stir on a low flame until cooked, adding the raisins and cashews last. This should take approximately 15 minutes and you should get a pulpy, chutney like mass. You may need to add a little more water. Add the aubergine slices to the pan. Stir once, cover and cook until soft (about 5-10 minutes). Serve at room temperature with hot tandoori roti. Can be refrigerated and eaten cold as a relish.

Mahashas
(Vegetables Filled with Savoury Rice)

This is a Baghdadi Jewish recipe which I learned from the Iny family who still have their family home in Colaba in Mumbai. Their food is essentially Middle Eastern but because the community has been in India for over two hundred years, many dishes have taken on a spicy feel. The stuffing is traditionally rice and chicken. Since there are no Kosher butchers left in Bombay, no meat or chicken is cooked in the Iny home anymore. Diana Iny replaces minced chicken in the original recipe with lapshi or burghul (cracked wheat) in the stuffing. Lapshi is both nutritious and very tasty. It also makes the dish hundred per cent vegetarian.

Serves 8

Ingredients

Vegetables for stuffing:

The most popular vegetables used for this dish are tomato, brinjal, zucchini, ridge or snake gourd, capsicum, cabbage, onion, spinach. Use medium sized vegetables.

Filling:

1 cup rice
1 cup lapshi (burgul)
½ tsp turmeric
1 tsp salt
½ tsp fresh grated ginger
1 tsp crushed garlic
½ tsp powdered cinnamon
½ cup chopped fresh mint
½ cup lemon juice
5 tsp sugar
2 cups tomato juice
3 green chillies chopped

dash of tomato ketchup (optional)
dash of sweet chilli garlic sauce (commercial variety)

Method

Soak rice and lapshi for ½ hour in plenty of water, and then drain. Place all the ingredients into a bowl and mix well. Reserve ½ cup of tomato juice for later use.

For tomatoes, brinjal, capsicum and zucchini cut a slice from the top and scoop out gently. Fill only 2/3 full so there will be space for the rice to swell. Replace cut slice as a lid.

For onion mahashas, peel the onion and make a slit on one side until the center. Place onions in a pan, cover with water and bring to a boil. Cook for a few minutes only. The onions should be pliable and not too soft. Drain and cool the onions and separate the layers. Each layer is then stuffed with a tablespoon of filling and then loosely rolled. Alternatively roast the onions first and then remove the layers.

For cabbage and spinach, remove stalks and blanch leaves for a few seconds in boiling water. When the leaves are pliable, drain and add iced water to them in order to retain the colour and prevent further cooking. Place each leaf on a plate and place approximately 1 tablespoon of the filling on the leaf and roll while turning in the sides.

In a large, heavy bottomed handi, pour ½ cup of tomato juice. Place the vegetables in a single layer. Add ½ cup of water, cover with a tight lid and cook on medium heat for approximately 1 hour until cooked or bake in a medium oven in a roasting pan, covered.

The quantity of filling mixture should make you 20-24 mahashas.

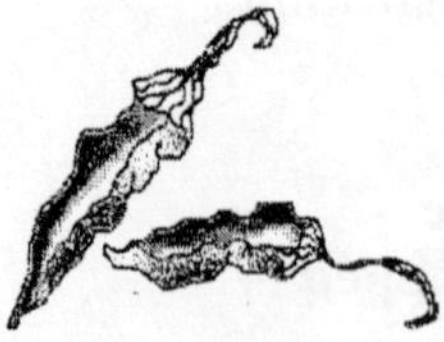

North India

My Aloo Methi
(Potatoes with Fenugreek)

Serves 4

Ingredients

6 tomatoes
6-8 cloves garlic, crushed
3-4 green chillies, slit
2 cups potatoes, parboiled and cut into 1" pieces
1 cup fresh fenugreek leaves
salt to taste

Method

Blanch and peel the tomatoes. Puree in a blender until smooth. Put them in a kadhai or wok with the garlic and green chillies and cook until you get the consistency of a thick sauce. The cooking time will vary according to the water content of the tomatoes but shouldn't take more than 7-10 minutes. Add the potatoes, fenugreek, a little water and salt. Simmer and cook covered for another 10 minutes or until the potatoes are soft, the gravy thick and the fenugreek leaves cooked but still green.
Serve hot with chapatis.

Sindhi

Sai Bhaji

Serves 6

Ingredients

3 bunches or 500g spinach, washed and chopped
3 onions, chopped
2" piece ginger, chopped
6 garlic cloves, chopped
3 tomatoes, blanched, skinned and chopped
1 cup red pumpkin, peeled and chopped
1 small brinjal, chopped
1 potato, peeled and chopped
1 carrot peeled and chopped
½ cup chickpea dal, soaked in water for at least 2 hours, water drained
2 tbsp fresh fenugreek or dill
4-6 green chillies chopped
salt to taste

Method

Put all the ingredients except the spinach into a large vessel with ½ cup water and cook until all the vegetables are soft and pulpy (may take 40-45 minutes in an ordinary vessel, 15 minutes in a pressure cooker). Mix well. Add the chopped spinach and continue stirring until all the excess water has evaporated and the spinach is just cooked. Mix well again until you get a thick mashed consistency. No individual vegetable should be visible. This does not look particularly pretty but it is delicious.

Traditionally, all the vegetables are cooked together. I like to add the spinach at the end to preserve its colour, flavour and nutritional value. Sai bhaji was originally one of those 'left over' dishes.

It is excellent with brown rice or roasted onion rice.

Corn in Creamy Milk

Serves 6

Ingredients

4 fresh corn cobs, preferably sweet corn
1 tsp salt
a pinch of sugar
2 tbsp fresh grated coconut or ½ cup coconut milk
1" piece of ginger
4 green chillies
4 tbsp fresh coriander, chopped
2 tsp mustard seeds
8 curry leaves
½ cup milk
salt to taste
2 tbsp yogurt, whipped
1 tbsp chopped coriander

Method

Put the corn cobs in a pan with enough water to cover. Add 1 teaspoon salt and a pinch of sugar to cook the corn. This is often more efficient in a pressure cooker. Sweet corn, however, is so tender that it only takes around 7 to 10 minutes in an ordinary pan. Remove the corn and break each one into about 3 to 4 chunks. Don't throw away the water in which they were boiled. Grind the coconut, ginger, green chillies and coriander with as little water as possible. If you are using coconut milk, then use a blender not a grinder or grinding stone. Add this paste to the water from the corn (the water should be around 1 cup at least). Roast the mustard seeds and throw them into the pan along with the curry leaves. Stir and simmer. Add the corn. Cover and simmer for at least 10 minutes.
Pour in the milk and stir. Season. Add the yogurt just before serving.
Serve hot with plain boiled rice and garnish with chopped coriander.

Pulses & Rice

Fragrant Coconut Rice

Serves 8

Ingredients

2½ cups basmati or any long grained rice
10-12 curry leaves
1 tsp black peppercorn, whole
1 tsp cloves
2 lemon grass stalks cut into 1" pieces, bruised
2 tsp salt
4½ cups coconut milk
2 bay leaves
2 cups water

Method

Traditionally the rice is fried first with the spices before the coconut milk is added. I boil all the spices (uncovered) with the coconut milk and 2 cups water until the flavours are infused. Simmer and add the rice and salt and cook covered with a tight lid for approximately 20 minutes or until all the coconut milk has been absorbed. If the coconut milk is too creamy, you may need to add some water. Fork the rice lightly before serving.

Maharashtra

Masala Bhath (Savoury Rice)

Serves 4

Ingredients

1 cup Ambe Mor or any good quality rice
2 cups or more hot water
¼ cup Indian gherkin, peas or sliced cashews
2 tsp Deccan spice (pg. 33)
salt to taste
a squeeze of lime juice
1 tsp jaggery

Grind together the following to make a masala paste
2 tbsp grated dry coconut (roasted golden)
¼ tsp cumin seeds
1 green chilli

Roast together
A few curry leaves
½ tsp black mustard seeds
a pinch of asafoetida
¼ tsp turmeric

For garnishing
1 tsp chopped green coriander

Method

Roast together curry leaves, mustard, asafoetida and turmeric in an oven, a frying pan or on a tawa until the mustard begins to pop. Transfer to a handi or casserole and add the rice, 2 cups hot water and salt to taste. Add the vegetable or cashews, the ground masala paste, the Deccan spice, salt to taste and stir on a low flame. Add a squeeze of lemon juice and the jaggery. Cook covered until the rice is soft. Add the roasted spices and stir into the rice. Garnish with coriander. Serve with a raita or plain yogurt.

South India

Curd Rice

Serves 4

Ingredients

1 cup basmati rice
1 cup natural yogurt
1 tsp salt
2 green chillies chopped fine
½" piece of ginger, grated
½ tsp black mustard seeds
½ tsp of white dal
10 curry leaves
2 Kashmiri chillies roasted and crushed
1 tbsp fresh green coriander finely chopped
1 tsp vegetable oil
2½ cups water

Method

Cook the rice with the water until slightly soft. Drain if there is any water left and while the rice is hot, add the yogurt, salt, green chillies and ginger. Heat the oil in a small frying pan, put in the mustard seeds, white dal, curry leaves and red chillies in that order. When the chillies start to change colour remove from the fire and sprinkle over the rice and yogurt mixture. Stir in the coriander. Place in a mould. Press firmly with the back of a spoon and refrigerate. The mould can be a simple katori or bowl. Serve cold (not chilled) or at room temperature. Serve unmoulded as an accompaniment to any south Indian vegetable with papad. Can also be served as a starter with roasted papad and pickle.

Karwar

Chitra Anna (Lemon Rice)

Serves 6

Ingredients

2 cups rice — thick, unpolished varieties are best
1 tbsp mustard seeds
a pinch of asafoetida
1 tsp turmeric
2-3 red chillies broken into pieces
2 tbsp yellow split peas
1 cup peanuts
½ cup coconut, freshly grated
10-12 curry leaves
1 tsp ginger juliennes
¼ cup coriander, freshly chopped
salt to taste
1/3 cup lime juice
7½ cups water
rind of 1 lime
1 tsp ghee or oil

Method

Prepare masala by roasting sequentially the mustard, asafoetida, turmeric, chillies, yellow split pea, peanuts, grated coconut and curry leaves. Put them all into a handi along with the fresh coriander and ginger and stir with 1 teaspoon oil until you get a dry roasted flavour.
Wash the rice. Add 7½ cups of water and cook until all the water is absorbed. Keep adding water if necessary until the rice is almost cooked. Remove the handi and spread immediately on a cloth so that the rice doesn't get sticky. When almost cool, put the rice back into a bowl and add the roasted masala. Stir well. Add salt, lemon juice and lemon

rind. Can be served as is or re-heated in a microwave or on a very low gas. Do not reheat on a high gas flame, as the lemon rind will turn bitter. This also makes a perfect summer dish, served at room temperature with ladyfinger raita. The rice can also be moulded into a jelly mould. In this case, do not spread the rice on the cloth to cool and separate. Add the roasted masala, lemon juice and other ingredients to the hot rice. Wait for a few minutes for the rice to settle before unmoulding. Mix well, spoon into the mould and compress with a spoon. Place the raita in the well in the middle of the mould. Serve at room temperature.

Roasted Onion Rice

Serves 6

Ingredients

2 cups rice
6 onions, roasted
1 tsp oil
1" stick cinnamon
3-4 cloves
2-3 black cardamom
4½ cups water
Salt to taste

Method

Place whole onions in a hot oven. Brush with a little oil and roast on a low to medium temperature until they are golden and soft (around 30-40 minutes). Remove. Cool and discard only the outer skin (which should be charred). Chop the soft onion. Wash rice and place in a pan with the roasted onions, cinnamon, cloves, cardamom, water and salt. Cook covered until the rice is done. Add more water if necessary. Serve hot.

Goa

Feijoada

(Goan Style Beans)

Serves 5

Ingredients

1 cup, black eyed beans
2 onions, chopped fine
2 tomatoes, peeled and chopped
4 cloves garlic crushed coarsely
a pinch of turmeric
1 tbsp tamarind pulp
½ tsp ginger paste
1 tsp mild red chilli powder
1 cup coconut milk
salt to taste

Method

Soak the beans overnight. Wash in several changes of water. Cover with fresh water. Add the onions and cook until the beans are soft. You should have about 1 cup of water left in the pan after boiling. Add the tomatoes, garlic paste, turmeric, tamarind pulp, ginger paste and chilli powder and stir on a slow fire for about 10 minutes. Add the coconut milk and salt to taste. Simmer on a low flame until the gravy thickens.

Lemon dal

Serves 6

Ingredients

1 medium sized onion, sliced
2" piece cinnamon
2 cups orange dal, washed
3 garlic cloves, whole
1 tbsp chopped ginger
7½ cups stock (vegetable or chicken)
salt to taste
4 tbsp lime juice, plus 1 tbsp grated rind
1 green chilli, chopped
2 tbsp chopped fresh coriander leaves

Method

Put the sliced onion, cinnamon, dal, garlic, ginger and stock into a pan. Add salt. Bring to a boil, then simmer for about 20 minutes. Add the lime juice and cook for a further 10 minutes, stirring often. Add the chillies and rind just before serving. Alternatively, the entire operation can be done in a pressure cooker, adding the lemon juice, rind and chillies last. Garnish with chopped coriander leaves and serve hot.

Maharashtra

Maharashtrian Style Dal

Serves 4

Ingredients

1 cup yellow or orange dal
4 cups water
¼ tsp fenugreek seeds
½ tsp black mustard seeds
a pinch of asafoetida
2 green chillies chopped
a few curry leaves
¼ tsp turmeric
2-3 tsp Deccan Spice (pg. 33)
¼ tsp red chilli powder
5 pieces kokum
1 heaped tbsp jaggery
salt to taste
fresh, chopped coriander for garnish
water

Method

Cook the dal until soft with approximately 4 cups water. Mash roughly. Meanwhile roast ingredients from fenugreek to turmeric in an oven or on a tawa. Add to the dal. Throw in the Deccan spice, red chilli powder, kokum and jaggery. Add salt to taste, bring to a boil once (you may have to add a little water) and simmer for a few minutes until all the flavours are well absorbed.
Garnish with fresh coriander.

Konkan

Usal

Serves 8

Ingredients

½ kg black or brown chickpeas or black-eyed beans
10 cloves garlic, coarsely crushed
1 onion
Salt to taste

Grind the following into a fine paste:
2 tsp Malabar masala (pg. 32)
2 tbsp fresh coriander
10 garlic cloves
½ tsp turmeric powder
½ cup grated coconut or 1 cup coconut milk

Method

Soak the beans overnight. Drain water. Wash in several changes of water. Add fresh water to just cover the beans and cook with the garlic and one whole onion, until the beans are just done. Add salt and the masala paste to the beans and their liquid and cook further until you get a stew like consistency (about 10 minutes). Serve with a crunchy salad like carrot peanut and raisin.

Instead of dried beans, sprouted beans are a healthy substitute. In this case, you do not have to soak them overnight. Just add water to cover the sprouts. Mix in the masala paste, onion (chopped) and garlic and bring to a boil. Simmer until you get a stew like consisteney (about 10 minutes).

Non-Vegetarian

Main Course

Simple Goa Fish Curry

Serves 6

Ingredients

1 kg any firm white fish, sliced
1 tbsp cumin seeds
8 dry red chillies
½ tsp turmeric
½" piece ginger
6 cloves garlic
1 onion, chopped
2 green chillies, slit lengthways
4 cups water
1 tbsp tamarind pulp
3 cups coconut milk
salt to taste

Method

Grind the cumin seeds, red chillies, turmeric, ginger and garlic along with a little water into a fine paste. Put the masala paste, chopped onion and chillies along with 4 cups water into a large kadhai or wok. Bring to boil and simmer until the onions are soft. Add the tamarind pulp and coconut milk and heat through. Do not boil. Add the fish. Simmer until the fish is cooked (approximately 10-12 minutes). Add salt to taste.

Serve with plain boiled rice.

Goa

Very Simple Fish Curry

Serves 4

Ingredients

4 slices fish
salt to taste
1 tbsp lemon juice
1 onion chopped
1 tbsp Ambotik masala (pg. 33)
1 cup water
1 cup coconut milk
1 tbsp fresh coriander leaves

Method

Sprinkle the fish with salt and lemon juice. Set aside for 15 minutes. Boil together the onion, ambotik masala and 1 cup of water until the water has almost evaporated and you are left with a thick masala paste. Add the coconut milk and simmer. Drain the excess liquid from the fish and add to the curry just before serving.

Garnish with coriander and serve with plain boiled rice.

Coastal

Malabar Fish

Serves 6

Ingredients

1 kg firm, white fish, cleaned and cut into slices. If you use a filet of rawas, you can cut it into large chunks since it will have no bones.
¼ cup tamarind pulp
salt to taste
4 green chillies, slit
4 cups coconut milk

Grind the following to a fine paste
½ fresh coconut, grated
3 tsp Malabar masala (pg. 32)
½ tsp turmeric powder
10 cloves garlic, coarsely crushed

To garnish
1 tbsp fresh green coriander

Method

Put the masala paste on a slow flame with a little water until it changes colour (7 to 10 minutes). If it sticks add a little more water. Add the tamarind pulp, salt to taste, green chillies and lastly the coconut milk. Heat through once, add the fish until it is just cooked (approximately 15 minutes) and serve with hot rice. Garnish with coriander.

Parsee

Patra Ni Macchi

Serves 6

Ingredients

6 slices of pomfret ½" thick
3 banana leaves or aluminum foil
2 cups water
2 tbsp sugarcane vinegar

For the coconut chutney grind together the following to a smooth paste

the white of one coconut
5 green chillies, de-seeded
1 cup coriander leaves
½ cup mint leaves
1 whole head of garlic, peeled
½" piece of ginger
1 tsp roasted cumin seeds
4 tbsp lime juice
1 tsp sugar
salt to taste

Method

Cut the banana leaves into six large pieces, removing the center stem, (alternatively cut pieces of foil to fit each piece of fish). Pass the banana leaves quickly over a gas flame to soften them. Layer the chutney on each slice of fish and place on a piece of banana leaf or foil. Fold the leaves over to completely cover the fish and form a parcel. You may need to use two pieces of leaf per slice of fish in order to cover the fish properly. Tie the parcels with ordinary thread and set aside. Heat water and vinegar together in the bottom part of a steamer or a large pan. Place the fish in a steamer or in a colander over the pan. Steam for approximately 20 minutes.

Unwrap the parcels at the time of serving only. This is a lean version of the Parsee favourite.

Bengali in Inspiration

Fish Parcels with Mustard Sauce

Serves 6

Ingredients

1 kg of fish cut into 1" thick steaks or slices (rawas or any fish with firm white flesh)
1½ tsp salt
3 tbsp lime juice
3 tbsp fresh orange juice
4 heaped tbsp whole grain mustard
2 tbsp thick yogurt
2 Kashmiri chillies roasted and roughly chopped
1 tsp fennel seeds roasted and powdered
a pinch of sugar

Method

Wash and pat the fish dry. Sprinkle the fish with salt, lime and orange juice and marinate for at least 1 hour. Drain the marinade and place each steak on a banana leaf or foil. (See Patra ni Macchi). Mix together the mustard, yogurt, chilli, and fennel seeds. Smother each steak with this mixture equally and close the parcels tight. Bake in a moderate oven for 15-20 minutes. You will have to judge the cooking time according to the type of fish. Open the parcels only on the table. Serve with south Indian style potatoes and a green salad.

South India

Tamarind Fish

Serves 4

Ingredients

4 fillets of mackerel
1 tsp salt
2 tbsp tamarind pulp
1 tsp Kashmiri chilli powder
2 tsp ginger paste
2 tsp garlic paste
½ cup fresh chopped coriander
a little oil for brushing the aluminum foil

Method

Rub the salt into the mackerel fillets and set aside for 10 minutes. Remove any excess water. Mix the tamarind pulp, chilli powder, ginger and garlic paste. Rub this marinade all over the fish and marinate for at least 1 hour. Brush aluminum foil with a little oil to prevent sticking. Place the fillets on it. Grill the fish for about 7 minutes on each side or until lightly browned. Garnish with fresh coriander. Can be served hot with curd rice or cold as a starter.

This is a wicked deviant of the traditional recipe.

Sindhi

Fish with Fenugreek (Methi Macchi)

Serves 4

Ingredients

500g fish slices
salt to taste
3 tbsp lime juice
2 cups spinach, washed and cut
2 cups fresh fenugreek leaves
2 onions
8-10 cloves garlic, peeled but left whole
2-3 tomatoes, peeled and chopped
3 green chillies
1 tsp coriander powder
1 tsp cumin powder
¼ tsp turmeric
½ tsp red chilli powder

Method

Wash the fish and marinate with salt and lemon juice. Keep aside for 30 minutes. Meanwhile, puree the spinach, fenugreek, onions, garlic, tomatoes and green chillies in a blender until smooth. Put this paste unto a vessel and cook on a low flame, stirring continuously until thick. Add the coriander, cumin, turmeric and red chilli powder. Check seasoning. Drain the fish and pat dry. Add to the puree. Stir once and cook covered on a low flame until the gravy thickens and sticks to the fish (about 12-15 minutes).

You can also do the whole process in a heatproof dish in the oven. If there is any excess liquid in the dish, cook uncovered just before serving to dry up the water.

Prawn Balchao

Serves 6-8

Ingredients

1 kg medium sized prawns (shelled and deveined)
½ tsp turmeric
1" piece ginger
12 cloves garlic
1 tsp mustard seeds
8 red Kashmiri chillies
½ tsp cumin seeds
1 tsp sugar
1 tbsp dried shrimps
½ cup vinegar
2 large onions, chopped fine
1 cup water
salt to taste
2 tbsp tomato puree

Method

Grind turmeric, ginger, garlic, mustard, chillies, cumin seeds, sugar and dried shrimps to a fine paste with the vinegar. Cook the ground masala paste with the chopped onions in ½ cup of water. Stir continuously on a low flame until cooked. Add the prawns, salt and another ½ cup of water. Cook on a high flame for 5 minutes only until the prawns are cooked. Add the tomato puree. Mix thoroughly. Prawn balchao will keep for several days outside the fridge provided that the prawns are well cooked. I would suggest that you refrigerate this version since it has no oil. It can be eaten as a main course or as a pickle.

Goan Prawn Curry with Okra

Serves 6

Ingredients

500g raw prawns, peeled and deveined
200g okra topped and tailed with one vertical slit
4-5 pieces kokum
1 cup coconut milk thin (milk)
2½ cups coconut milk thick (cream)
(If you are using canned or ready made coconut milk add 3:1 ratio coconut milk to water for thin coconut milk.)
salt to taste

Grind to a fine paste with a little water the following:
10 dry Kashmiri chillies
1 tsp black pepper corns
1 tsp cumin seeds
¼ tsp turmeric powder
10 medium cloves of garlic
1 piece of ginger
2 tsp sesame seeds
salt to taste

Method

Put the ground/paste masala into a heavy-bottomed pan with the thin coconut milk. Cook on a very low gas flame and slowly stir until the masala cooks, which would take about 7-10 minutes. It should change to a deep brown/red colour. Add the thick coconut milk a little at a time until it is all incorporated. Throw in the kokum and simmer. Add the prawn and okra just before serving and heat through once. Add salt to taste. Never boil the curry as the oil from the coconut milk will separate and come to the surface.
The same masala can be used for fish curry but the okra must be omitted. The fish should be sprinkled with salt and drained of excess water before adding to the curry. Serve with plain boiled rice and dry prawn relish. For a milder curry, add 1 more cup of coconut milk towards the end of cooking.

Prawn or Fish Caldin

Serves 6

Ingredients

500g firm white fish sliced into ¾" slices or 500g prawns after peeling and deveining
2 medium sized onions, thinly sliced
4 cups coconut milk
1 tbsp tamarind pulp or ½ raw mango cut into thin strips
salt to taste

Grind the following to a fine paste with water
10 mild green chillies
½ tsp turmeric powder
6 garlic cloves
2 tbsp fresh coriander
1 tbsp ginger, chopped
1 tsp black peppercorns
1 tsp cumin seeds
1 tsp whole coriander seeds
2 tbsp khus khus (white poppy seeds)
1 cup water
To garnish: a few slit green chillies

Method

Put the onions and the masala along with 1 cup of water on a low flame and cook until the onions are soft and you are left with a thick paste (about 7-10 minutes). If the masala sticks, you may need to add a little more water. Pour in the coconut milk a little at a time. Next, add the tamarind or raw mango and simmer for at least 10 minutes. Throw in the prawns or fish just before serving. Check for salt. Garnish with a few slit green chillies. Serve with hot rice.

Malabar Crab

Serves 4

Ingredients

1 kg black mud crab, cleaned and cut into large pieces
1 onion, roasted
8 cloves garlic, roasted
½ cup fresh or desiccated coconut, roasted
2 tbsp Malabar masala (pg. 32)
2 cups water
1 tbsp tamarind pulp
4 green chillies, slit lengthways

Method

Roast the onion and a whole garlic pod, on a tawa or griddle or in the oven (see glossary). Remove and slice the onion. Remove around 8 cloves of garlic and crush. Keep the roasted, grated coconut aside. Clean the crab by removing the stomach sac, gills etc. Wash the crabs. Crack the claws with the back of a knife to allow the masala to enter while cooking. In a large wok, put in the sliced onions, garlic and coconut. Stir fry for a few minutes. Add the Malabar masala, 2 cups of water and the crabs. Stir well. Cover the pan with a lid and cook on a medium flame until the crab pieces have turned pink. Add tamarind pulp and green chillies. You may need to stir several times while cooking. Depending on the size of the pieces, the crab should take around 15 to 20 minutes to cook. Remove the lid and if there is still quite a bit of liquid, cook on a high flame uncovered to dry up the liquid. This is a dry dish and the masala should cling to the crab. Never overcook crab since the flesh will turn rubbery. Taste for salt. If the crabs are sea and not the fresh water variety, there is usually no need to add salt at all.

Crabs should (preferably) always be bought live. This may seem a bit gruesome but it is the only way of ensuring that it is fresh. Once a crab is dead, the flesh disintegrates very quickly. How to kill the beast, you may ask? A tricky question. The coward's way out is to dunk the thing in boiling water for 5 to 10 minutes or until it stops moving, remove and then cook according to the recipe for 10 minutes less. This is satisfactory but some of the flavour does get lost in the water. If you are brave (or have someone brave around like I do), break the claws off while the beast is alive. It is possible. The rest is not so gruesome!

Stuffed Crabs

Serves 6

Ingredients

8 small black crabs
½ cup vinegar
1 onion, finely chopped
8 cloves garlic, finely chopped
2" piece ginger, finely chopped
½ tsp turmeric
5 green chillies finely chopped
3 tomatoes chopped fine
1 tsp lemon juice
salt to taste
2 tsp fresh coriander finely chopped
½ tsp garam masala

Method

Wash the fresh crabs and remove the shells. Place the shells in a large vessel and pour in enough water to cover. Add ½ cup vinegar to the water and boil for five minutes or until the shells turn pink. Remove from the water and wipe dry. Boil the remaining crabs for 5-10 minutes. Cool. Remove all the crabmeat by breaking the claws and body (this is the tedious bit). Cook the chopped onion and garlic in ½ cup water until cooked but not soft. Add ginger, turmeric, chillies and tomatoes and cook for a further five minutes until thick. Add the crab meat, lemon juice, salt and chopped coriander and toss for just a minute. Add the garam masala. Stir for 2 minutes.

Remove from the heat and serve in the crab shells. Can be served hot or cold as a starter. You can also dust the stuffed crabs with seasoned breadcrumbs and grill before serving.

Singapore

Pepper Crabs

Freshly crushed pepper has a flavour that is unmatched. I prefer to crush them when required than to crush and store in bottles for later use.

Serves 6

Ingredients

1 kg crab
10 cloves garlic (unpeeled and crushed coarsely)
1 stalk lemon grass (minced)
4 green chillies (smashed coarsely)
salt to taste
1 cup water or chicken stock
4 tbsp pepper (freshly ground) or coarsely crushed

Method

Clean and wash the crabs. Chop into pieces and keep aside.(See Malabar Crab for cleaning instructions.) Put the garlic, lemon grass and chilli in a wok or large kadahi with the water or stock. Cook until it smells fragrant (7-10 minutes). Add the crab pieces and salt, stir-fry for 5 minutes. Sprinkle all the pepper and cook covered for another 10 minutes or until the crab turns pink / orange, which means that it is cooked. The spices should cling to the crab pieces.

Squid Ambotik

Serves 4

Ingredients

500g squid, cleaned and cut into rings (rounds)
2 medium sized onions, chopped
6 cloves garlic chopped
1 tomato, chopped
2 green chillies, slit lengthwise
2 tbsp Ambotik masala (pg. 33)
1 cup water
salt to taste

Method

To clean the squid, twist off the head and tentacles. Pull out the inner plastic like cartilage. You will be left with a tube like body. Pull off the purple brown skin from the outside of the body. Wash the squid thoroughly. Dry on towels and cut into ¼" thick rings. Like prawns and fish, if the squid is fresh it will not smell fishy at all.

For a lean cuisine dish of squid, put the onions, garlic, tomato, chillies and ambotik masala into a pan with 1 cup of water. Reduce to a thick paste or gravy. Add the squid. Adjust the salt and cook on a medium heat until the squid turns just white which should take about 5-7 minutes. Take care not to overcook the squid as it turns rubbery very quickly. Serve warm as a starter with a green salad.

Goa

Stuffed Mackerels

Serves 4

Ingredients

4 large mackerels (bangda), washed and gutted
2 tsp salt
4 tbsp lime juice
4 tbsp Ambotik masala (pg. 33)
1 tsp oil for brushing

Method

Make a couple of slashes in each fish and rub salt and lime juice all over them. Leave to marinate for at least 20 minutes. Drain and stuff each fish with 1 tablespoon of the Ambotik masala. Make sure that the masala enters all the slits have to marinate for 30 minutes. Then place under a hot grill. Cook for 5-7 minutes on each side. Brush with a little oil to prevent sticking.

Traditionally, mackerels are dusted with rice flour and shallow fried on both sides.

Parsee

Eggs on Tomatoes

Serves 6

Ingredients

1 kg tomatoes, blanched, peeled & chopped
5 onions, chopped
1 stick of cinnamon
2-3 cloves
1 tbsp garlic paste
2 tsp chilli powder
½ cup fresh coriander chopped
salt to taste
1½ tsp sugar
3 tbsp malt vinegar
1 tbsp Worcestershire sauce
6 eggs

Method

Put the tomatoes, onions, cinnamon, cloves, garlic and chilli into a heavy bottomed pan and simmer until the sauce thickens. Depending on the tomatoes, this could take anywhere from 10 to 20 minutes. Add fresh coriander, salt and cook for a further 5-10 minutes until the tomatoes are reduced to a thick puree. Add the sugar, vinegar and Worcestershire sauce, and allow to cook for a couple more minutes to blend the flavours. Remove the pan from the heat. Discard the cinnamon and cloves. Spread the mixture evenly into an oven proof dish. Make six depressions in the mixture with the back of a spoon. Carefully break an egg into each depression. Cover with foil and bake in a medium oven until the eggs have just set. Serve immediately.
A lean version of the Parsee favourite.

Chicken Steaks Goan Style

Serves 6

Ingredients

6 chicken breasts
½ cup yogurt
1 tbsp coriander seeds, ground
½ tsp cumin seeds, ground
½ tsp black mustard seeds, ground
½ tsp turmeric, ground
½ tsp Kashmiri chilli powder
1 tbsp lemon juice
1½ tsp salt

For garnishing

boiled baby onions and potatoes

Method

Using a mallet, flatten the chicken breasts to about ¼" thick. Whisk the yogurt until smooth and add the spices and salt. Mix well. Spread all over the chicken and marinate for 2 hours. Arrange the chicken in an ovenproof dish. Bake in a moderate oven for 15 minutes. Turn over and continue baking for a further 10 minutes. Garnish with boiled baby onions and potatoes. Sprinkle the lemon juice over the chicken before serving.

Goa

Chicken Indad

Serves 6

Ingredients

1 kg chicken cut into 10 pieces
8 dry red chillies
1 tbsp peppercorns
½ tsp turmeric
12 cloves garlic
½ tsp cumin seeds
1 ½" piece ginger
1 large onion
1 tbsp tamarind paste
3 tbsp vinegar
1 tbsp oil
3" piece cinnamon
6 whole cardamon
5 whole cloves

Method

Grind into a paste the dry red chillies, peppercorns, turmeric, garlic, cumin, ginger, onion, tamarind and vinegar. Fry the chicken in 1 tablespoon oil with the cinnamon (broken into pieces), cardamon and cloves. A nonstick pan would help. Add the ground masala and keep mixing until the masala looses its raw smell. You will need to add a cup or two of water. Cover and cook until the chicken is tender. It will take approximately 25 minutes. This dish is almost dry and can be served as a starter or a main course.

Konkan

Malvani Chicken

Serves 4

Ingredients

1 kg chicken, cut into 6-8 pieces

2 large onions roasted, and cut into rough slices (see glossary)

3 tsp Malabar masala (pg. 32)

1 cup grated coconut, roasted on a griddle until golden

2 cups water or chicken stock

Grind to a fine paste the following

1 green chilli

1" piece of ginger

½ cup fresh coriander

1 small onion, roasted

¼ tsp turmeric

3 cloves of garlic, roasted

salt to taste

Method

Apply the masala paste to the chicken and marinate for at least one hour. Put the chicken into a large pan or handi. Add the roasted onions, Malabar masala, coconut and 2 cups water or stock. Stir well. Bring to a boil and then simmer until the chicken is cooked, which will take approximately 40 to 50 minutes if you slow cook it. You should get the consistency of a thick gravy.

Serve hot with rice bhaakri (flat rotis made of ground rice) or crusty bread.

Burma

Kauswe
(Burmese Chicken Curry with Noodles)

Serves 6-8

Ingredients

1½ kg chicken, cut into pieces
5 cloves garlic, chopped
3 medium onions, chopped
1 tbsp ginger, chopped
1 tsp cumin powder
1 tsp coriander seeds roasted and crushed
4 tbsp tomato puree
½ cup water
1-2 tsp chilli powder
2 tsp salt
2 cups thin coconut milk
2 cups thick coconut milk
500g thin egg noodles
1 cup water

Method

Put garlic, onion, ginger, cumin and coriander into blender and blend until smooth. Put into a wok along with the tomato puree and 1 cup water. Bring to a boil and simmer until the masala is cooked. Add the chicken and coat with the masala. Add chilli powder, salt and thin coconut milk. Simmer until chicken is tender and bring slowly to just under a boil, stirring constantly to prevent the mixture from curdling. Add the thick coconut milk. Stir. Check seasoning.

Just before serving, cook noodles in a large pan of boiling salted water until just tender. Transfer them to a pan of cold water to stop the cooking and then drain the noodles in a colander.

Serve the noodles in soup plates. Pour over the Kauswe and leave guests to top with whichever accompaniments they like. The curry should not be very thick. It should have a velvety smooth consistency and be mildly spicy.

Traditional accompaniments:

Finely sliced spring onions - both white and green portions
Chopped fresh coriander leaves
Roasted chickpeas, finely ground in a blender or a mortar
Crisp fried noodles broken into small pieces
Fried onion flakes
Thinly sliced garlic, fried in oil until golden
Lemon wedges
Dried chillies, roasted and broken or crushed
Chilli powder
Hardboiled eggs, halved

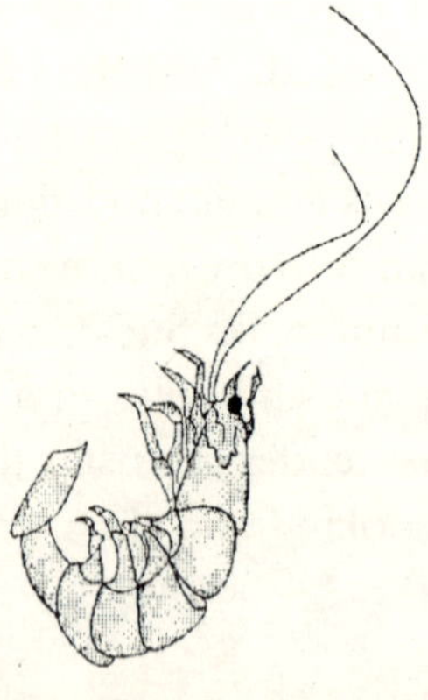

Goa

Pork or Mutton Chops

Serves 6-8

Ingredients

1 kg pork or mutton chops, fat trimmed completely
1" piece ginger
6 cloves garlic
2 green chillies
2 tsp salt
1 tsp whole cumin seeds
1 tsp garam masala
2 tsp black pepper, freshly ground
3 tbsp vinegar or lemon juice to grind the masala to a smooth paste

Method

Grind all the spices to a fine paste in the vinegar or lemon juice. For pork chop fanatics, this is a tasty and lean way of having your favourite meat. Take care to trim the fat off. Slightly flatten the chops with a mallet or the back of a large knife. Rub the paste over the chops and marinate for at least an hour. Steam cook in a pressure cooker for approximately 15 minutes or until the chops are soft. Alternatively place the chops in a heavy-bottomed vessel or terracotta pot. Add ½ cup of water, cover with a lid and slow cook for 40 minutes. (This marination can also be used for barbecue chops.) Brown the chops in the same masala on a high flame until golden on each side. There is enough fat in the meat to be able to do this. Serve hot with steamed vegetables.

Goa

Steaks

Serves 6-8

Ingredients

1 kg beef (undercut)
2 tbsp peppercorns
1 tbsp cumin seeds
1 tbsp ginger-garlic paste
1 tsp garam masala
2 tbsp vinegar
salt to taste

Method

Grind together the peppercorns, cumin seeds, ginger-garlic paste and garam masala in vinegar. Wash and trim the undercut of all fat. Cut into 1" thick slices against the grain and flatten with your hand, not with a mallet. Add salt and marinate in the above masala. Refrigerate overnight. Remove the steaks and place in a hot nonstick pan, which has been brushed with as little oil as possible. Dabbing a cloth or tissue paper in a little oil and coating the pan will do the trick. The pan must be very hot when you put the steaks in. Turn once to brown both sides. Serve immediately with a salad. Do not keep steaks hanging around as they will lose their precious juices. A rare steak will take 3-4 minutes to cook, medium rare approximately 6-7 minutes and well done will take approximately 10 minutes.

Maharashtra

Kolhapuri Mutton

Serves 4

Ingredients

½ kg lamb or mutton

Grind the following to a fine paste

2 large onions, sliced thin
½ cup coconut, grated, lightly roasted till golden
1 tsp garlic paste
1 tsp ginger paste
2 tbsp Kolhapuri masala (pg. 31)

For the meat

10 curry leaves
2 bay leaves
½ tsp turmeric
½ tsp ginger-garlic paste
1 onion chopped fine
1 cup water
salt to taste

To garnish

½ cup fresh, chopped coriander

Method

Grind onions, coconut, garlic paste, ginger paste and Kolhapuri masala to a fine masala paste. Set aside. Put the meat in a large skillet with the meat ingredients and 1 cup or more of water. (If you pressure cook, less water is needed and the meat should be tender in 15-20 minutes.) Cook until the meat is soft (around 40 minutes). Add the masala paste and salt. Mix well and simmer for about 15 minutes. The gravy should be thick and spicy. Garnish with chopped, fresh coriander.

Traditionally Kolhapuri mutton is served with bhaakri made from millet or sorghum. The ones made from millet are slightly heavier to digest. Millet is sometimes kneaded with sugarcane juice instead of water, which gives a hint of sweetness and takes the edge off the spice in this dish. Kolhapur is famous for this fiery number. But it has wonderful, light mutton dishes made in a white gravy, rather like a stew, too. Although this dish is representative of the spicy rich food of this area, the use of large amounts of spices in this dish was actually to mask the poor cuts of meat available to the common man during the reign of the Peshwas.

North India

Palak Gosht
(Mutton with Spinach)

Just as delicious and uses much less oil as neither the meat nor the spices are browned first. The flavour, nutritional value and colour of the spinach is also retained because it is added at the end of the cooking.

Serves 6

Ingredients

1 kg young mutton from the shoulder or leg, cut into chunks.
2 tbsp lime juice
salt to taste
1 tbsp freshly ground pepper
1" piece of ginger, crushed
6 garlic cloves, crushed
3 medium onions, finely chopped
5 whole cloves
4 green cardamom
2" stick cinnamon
3 green chillies finely chopped
1 tsp whole cumin seeds
½ tsp turmeric
1 tsp whole coriander seed
6 large tomatoes blanched, skinned, and chopped fine
1 cup water
3 bunches or 500g fresh spinach washed and chopped roughly (never use canned spinach, if you are desperate, frozen leaf spinach will do)
½ cup thick yogurt

Method

Marinate the meat in the lime juice, salt, pepper, ginger and garlic overnight if possible, but for at least for 2 hours. Put the onions, spices, meat and tomatoes together with 1 cup of water into a handi. Bring to a boil, simmer and cook covered until the meat is very soft (about 1 hour). Remove the lid and if there is still some liquid in the pan, continue to cook on a high flame. Add the spinach and cook for a further 5 minutes (no more, since the spinach must not darken) on a slow fire. Mix in the yogurt. Check seasoning. Serve with bhaakri or tandoori roti and raita.

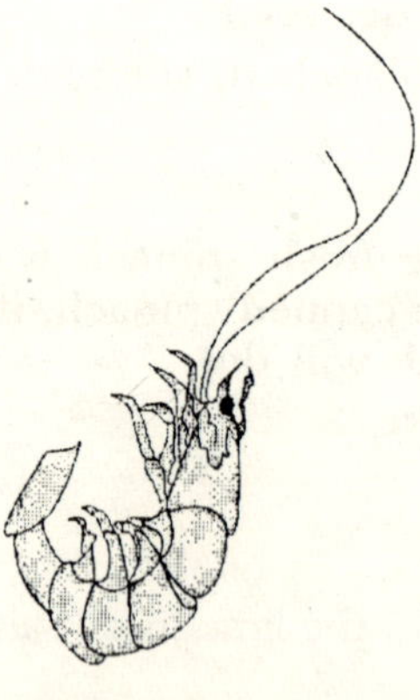

Kashmir

Yakhni

(Kashmiri Style Mutton with Yogurt)

Serves 6

Ingredients

1 kg young mutton (chest pieces), fat removed
a pinch of asafoetida
salt to taste
1½ tsp ginger powder
2½ tsp fennel seeds
3 black cardamom
3 cloves
2" stick cinnamon
3 cups water
2½ cups yogurt, slightly beaten

Method

Put all the ingredients except the yogurt in a heavy-bottomed pan. Add 3 cups of water and cook until the meat is tender (which would take approximately 45 minutes to 1 hour). Alternatively, pressure cook until the meat is tender. Whisk the yogurt until smooth with a balloon whisk or fork. Add to the mutton and heat the mixture slowly until it boils. Simmer for a further 10 minutes. Check seasoning and serve hot with white rice.

Desserts

Lean cuisine desserts are a difficult proposition. Stick to dried fruit which you wash, soak and poach in water, wine or fruit juice. Fresh tropical fruit (mangoes, melons, pineapple, papaya and passion fruit etc.) to which you can add a little candied ginger and lemon juice are always a good option as a dessert. Sorbets or 'gola' made with fresh juice are another light option to the end of a meal as are milk or yogurt based sweets where honey replaces white sugar.

South India

Rice Kheer

Serves 2

Ingredients

½ cup rice, ground fine
5 cups milk
sugar to taste
¼ tsp crushed cardamom (skin removed)
1/3 cup cashewnuts
2 tbsp raisins
1 tsp pistachios, crushed

Method

Soak the rice in water. Take one cup of milk and reduce to a brown flavourful paste (mawa). Add the remaining 4 cups of milk. Stir well. Drain the water from the rice and add to the milk along with the sugar and crushed cardamom. Cook for 20 minutes on a slow flame. Serve hot or cold garnished with crushed cashewnuts, raisins and pistachios.

Figs Poached with Red Wine & Tea

Serves 6

Ingredients

10 dried figs or 8 nos fresh figs
¾ cup brandy
¾ cup dry red wine or dry sherry
½ cup honey
½ tsp grated ginger
2 cloves
2" piece cinnamon
a few drops of vanilla essence
1/3 cup of strong tea, unsweetened
juice and zest of two oranges and two limes
1 cup whipped yogurt

Method

Wash the figs in warm water (cold water is preferable for fresh figs), drain and place in a bowl. Pour in the brandy, cover and leave overnight. Next morning remove the fruit from the brandy. Pour the brandy into a saucepan and add all the other ingredients and simmer for 30 minutes. Strain the mixture through a fine sieve. Return the syrup to the pan. Add the fruit. Place the pan on a low heat and simmer for about an hour or until the fruit is soft. The syrup should be the consitency of a thick, syrupy sauce. If it is too sweet add some more lemon juice. Serve the fruit with a little syrup and some whipped yogurt on the side.

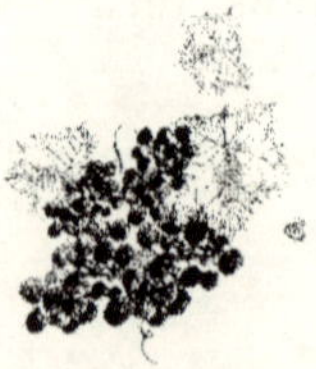

Peppered Pears in Wine

Serves 6

Ingredients

6 fresh pears
zest from one orange (This can be done with a good potato peeler)
½ bottle dry red wine
4½ tsp sugar
2" piece cinnamon
½ tsp black peppercorns
2 tbsp unsweetened yogurt per serving

Method

Peel the pears and place them upright in a stainless steel pan. If you have a corer, remove the core carefully first. In another pan, bring to boil the zest, wine, sugar, cinnamon and pepper. Reduce heat and simmer for five minutes. Pour this over the pears, cover with a lid and poach until tender (about 20 minutes). The wine mixture should cover the pears, upto the base of the stalk. Cool and remove the pears. Strain the syrup and boil rapidly until thick. Cool again and pour over the pears before chilling. Serve with whipped, unsweetened yogurt.

Remember that alcohol evaporates in cooking, leaving nothing behind but a few calories worth of sugar and tons of flavour.

Shrikhand

Serves 6

Ingredients

6½-7 cups yogurt
2 tbsp almonds
2 tbsp unsalted pistachios
½ cup honey
½ tsp ground cardamom
½ tsp saffron, dissolved in a little warm water
2 tbsp rosewater

Method

Pour the yogurt into the middle of a large piece of muslin, gather the corners together and tie them with a string or a rubber band and hang the muslin over a bowl for 2-3 hours to drain off the excess water. Meanwhile, drop the nuts in boiling water and cook for about 1 minute. Drain them well and rub off the skins with a cloth. Turn the yogurt into a bowl, add the honey and mix the two together thoroughly. Stir in the cardamom, saffron and rosewater. Turn into a large bowl or individual bowls and sprinkle with the nuts. Serve chilled.

Fresh fruit also tastes wonderful in this dish. Omit the rose water and the nuts and add 1 cup of mango or chikoo pulp to the mixture along with the honey. You don't have to mix it too well as it looks and tastes very attractive if it is marbled and the fruit is a distinct layer from the shrikhand. If the mango is too sweet, you may have to add a little lemon juice or cut down on the honey.

Fruit Salad with Mint and Preserved Ginger

Serves 6

Ingredients

1 small cantaloupe (green/orange melon) peeled, de-seeded and cut into 2"cubes

2 cups grapes (green or black), preferably seedless

2 cups fresh pineapple, cleaned and cut into 2"cubes

(any fruit can be used but those high in water content are preferable. Avoid bananas and apples)

2 tbsp ginger, finely chopped

juice of 1 lime

3 tbsp honey

1½ cup water

1 cup fresh mint leaves (whole, do not chop)

Method

Put the ginger, lemon juice, honey and water into a saucepan. Bring to a boil and simmer uncovered until the ginger is soft and the syrup has thickened (about 15 - 20 minutes). The syrup should have reduced by half. Cool and refrigerate. Add a few tablespoons of this to any fruit salad. The ginger brings out the delicate flavour and sweetness of melon and pineapple. It is also good with fresh figs and orange. Take care not to pour too much ginger syrup on the fruit, as it will overpower the fruity flavour. Pour over the fruit. Mix in the fresh mint and serve chilled.

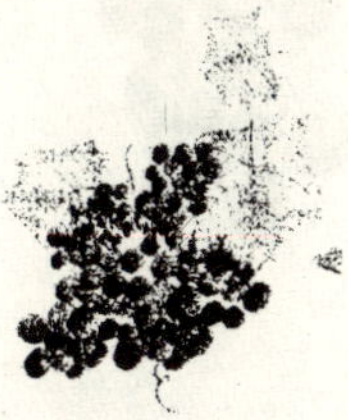

Index

somph = fennel